The Hello Reader! Activity Book

Instant Activities and Hands-on Reproducibles for Building Early Literacy Skills With 25 Favorite *Hello Readers!*

by Gina Shaw

SCHOLASTIC
PROFESSIONAL BOOKS

New York ■ Toronto ■ London ■ Auckland ■ Sydney

Dedication

To my wonderful, supportive, and enthusiastic
family—Jeff, Matt, Matt, and Brian!

Acknowledgments

To Terry Cooper and Liza Charlesworth, who
gave me the opportunity to write this book.

To Linda Beech—my first editor—
who had the patience to teach me how
to write for children and teachers.
It's been a treat to work with you once again.
Thank you for all of your terrific ideas
and for making this book come alive!

To Bernette Ford, Grace Maccarone,
and Edie Weinberg, who answered all
of my questions and who make coming
to the office every day a true joy!

And to all of the talented authors and
illustrators whom I have had the privilege
of working with on *Hello Reader!* books.

Scholastic Inc. grants teachers permission to photocopy the activity sheets
from this book for classroom use. No other part of this publication may be
reproduced in whole or part, or stored in a retrieval system, or transmitted
in any form or by any means, electronic, mechanical, or otherwise, without
written permission of the publisher. For information regarding permission,
write to Scholastic Inc., 555 Broadway, New York, NY 10012

Cover design by Jaime Lucero and Liza Charlesworth

Interior Design by Ellen Matlach Hassell
for Boultinghouse & Boultinghouse, Inc.

Interior art interpreted by Maxie Chambliss and Manuel Rivera

ISBN: 0-590-99611-8

Copyright © 1997 by Gina Shaw. All rights reserved.

Hello Reader! is a registered trademark of Scholastic, Inc.

Printed in the U.S.A.

10 9 8 7 6 5 4 3 2 1   7 8 9 / 00 / 01 / 02 / 03 / 04

Contents

Introduction

For 20 years, I have written and edited educational materials for teachers and children. Five years ago, I became part of the Cartwheel Books staff. I have been told that among the reasons I was hired was that I understood teachers' needs in the classroom as well as the kinds of books young children like to read. I was thrilled to join the Cartwheel staff since I knew that the *Hello Reader!* line—easy-to-read, beginning books for emerging readers—had just been started and all of the books that I had read in this series I loved.

That love affair continues today. Each and every *Hello Reader!* that I have edited holds a special meaning for me. I might love an author's manuscript because the rhyme is so good that I just have to read it out loud in my office; or because the theme is perfectly on-target for our young readers, or because the manuscript is so fanciful that it will take young children outside of themselves for a short while; or because I see the potential to use the book as a great teaching tool in the classroom. Of course, I also love working with all of the talented illustrators who bring visions to these books that I could never imagine. I am still awed by the entire publishing process—from manuscript to bound book!

My goal in writing this book is twofold—to make you feel the same way I do about *Hello Readers!* and to answer the many requests that have been made by teachers over the years to extend the use of *Hello Readers!* into their classrooms. I hope I have succeeded.

Ideas for using 25 of the *Hello Reader!* titles are included in this book. You'll find:

- topics for discussion
- cross-curricular suggestions
- manipulatives
- research assignments
- role-play ideas
- reading strategies
- hands-on learning activities
- crafts projects
- games
- recipes

and many other ideas for furthering the enjoyment of the *Hello Reader!* books.

How the Book Is Organized

The lessons follow the same format for each book. The sections include:

ABOUT THIS BOOK: a short summary of the *Hello Reader!* book.

THEMES: a list of the different classroom themes the book can be used with.

MEET THE AUTHOR AND ILLUSTRATOR: brief biographical notes and fun facts about each book's author and illustrator.

BOOK-RELATED ACTIVITIES: Before Reading activities that focus on a book's cover or children's prior knowledge; After Reading activities that extend learning.

ACTIVITIES FOR THE REPRODUCIBLES: You'll find two reproducibles for each *Hello Reader!* title. Students can work on these independently or in groups. This section also tells what skills the reproducibles cover and gives suggestions about materials to have on hand as children complete the pages. In some cases, there are extension activities based on the reproducibles.

MORE CROSS-CURRICULAR ACTIVITIES: This section is filled with ideas to relate each book to children's everyday lives, to themes they are learning in school, and to other curriculum areas. Many activities give children more practice in reading and writing; others just provide good fun.

Hello Reader! Background

Hello Reader! books come in five levels—*My First Hello Reader! With Flash Cards;* Level 1 for preschoolers to first graders (ages 3–6); Level 2 for kindergarteners to second graders (ages 5–7); Level 3 for first and second graders (ages 6–8); and Level 4 for second and third graders (ages 7–9). The activities in this book are based on Level 1, Level 2, and Level 3 *Hello Readers!*

The *Hello Reader!* line was started in 1991. It has always been the goal of Editorial Director Bernette Ford and Executive Editor Grace Maccarone to publish books that new readers will want to buy and read on their own. Every *Hello Reader!* must have a strong title and a popular subject as well as a topic that is meaningful to a four- to nine-year-old child. An appealing cover and colorful, attractive illustrations are essential.

In a *Hello Reader!* book, the main character usually has a problem that escalates. The stories have suspense and then a climax and resolution. Many of the stories are also humorous. The objective is to give new readers, who sometimes find reading a challenging task, a desire to keep going.

Familiar words and simple sentences also help beginning readers. Many of the stories are told with rhythm, rhyme, or repetition. Each *Hello Reader!* manuscript is tested for a readability level.

In addition to the original *Hello Reader!* books, your students might enjoy and learn from *Hello Science Readers!* and *Hello Math Readers!* Other mini-series in the line include *The First-Grade Friends* series, *The School Friends* series, *Invisible Inc.* (a mystery series), *Lad a Dog* (a series based on the original stories written by Albert Payson Terhune in the early 1900s), and *A Girl Named...* and *A Boy Named...* (a biography series). In other words, the entire line of *Hello Readers!* has something for everyone!

✖ How to Use *Hello Readers!*

You can use *Hello Readers!* with the whole class, in small groups, or for individual readers. When introducing a new *Hello Reader!*, start off by sharing comments about the cover. The Before Reading sections in this book suggest different activities to use with the covers.

At the beginning of every *Hello Reader!*, you'll find a note to parents from educational specialist Dr. Priscilla Lynch. Her advice also works well for the classroom teacher.

Research shows that reading books aloud is the single most valuable support that can be provided in helping young children learn to read. So feel free to read these books aloud to your students. Dr. Lynch also suggests:

- Be a ham! The more enthusiasm you display, the more your class will enjoy the book.

- Run your finger underneath the words as you read to signal that the print carries the story.

- Leave time for examining the illustrations more closely; encourage students to find details in the pictures.

- Invite youngsters to join in whenever there is a repeated phrase in the text.

- Link up events in the book with similar events in students' lives. (NOTE: The Activities for the Reproducibles and the More Cross-Curricular Activities in this book give suggestions for different kinds of activities.)

Dr. Lynch also points out that your attention and praise are absolutely crucial to students' continuing efforts to learn to read.

- If a student is learning to read and asks for a word, you might tell it to him or her so that the meaning of the story is not interrupted.

- Of course, if the student initiates the act of sounding out, it may be best not to intervene.

- Above all else, enjoy students' growing command of print and make sure you give lots of praise.

I hope both you and your students enjoy reading the *Hello Readers!* and working with them!

—Gina Shaw

"Buzz," Said the Bee

▪ About This Book

Once there was a bee who sat on a duck. "Quack," said the duck. "There's a bee on me." The duck said, "Scat!" But the bee just sat. So the duck sat on a hen, the hen sat on a pig, the pig sat on a cow, the cow sat on a sheep—until the bee finally said, "Buzzzzz," and all of the animals scampered away!

▪ Themes

This book ties in nicely with the following themes: **Animals** and **Farm Animals**.

▪ Meet the Author and Illustrator

Wendy Cheyette Lewison was working for a major publishing house when she sent this manuscript to Grace Maccarone, the executive editor of the *Hello Reader!* books. The *Hello Reader!* easy-to-read series was just getting started, and Lewison's book seemed ideal to help launch the line. *"Buzz," Said the Bee* still remains one of the best-selling books in this program.

One of the things that make this book so popular is the artwork by **Hans Wilhelm.** Although Wilhelm usually writes and illustrates his own books, he agreed to do the artwork for this title because he thought the book was delightfully funny. Among the titles Wilhelm has illustrated are *Hiccups for Elephant, Halloween Cats, Valentine Cats,* and the books in the *Dinofours* series.

▪ Book-Related Activities

BEFORE READING Show children the cover as you read the title aloud. Ask volunteers to identify the animals on the cover. Then ask children to tell you what sounds these animals make. Compile a list on the chalkboard of each animal and its sound.

AFTER READING Review the list of sounds you wrote on the chalkboard. Were these sounds used in the book? Choose children to take the parts of the different animals for a choral reading. Encourage students to make their sounds realistic. Choose a narrator to read the story, and have the "animals" contribute their sounds.

⠿ Activities for the Reproducibles

NAME THAT ANIMAL (Language Arts) Reproducible 1 helps students review vocabulary in the book. If children are having difficulty, encourage them to look back at the story. To extend this activity, have students think of other animals and write a rhyming sentence about each animal to add to the story.

WE SPEAK (Social Studies) Reproducible 2 increases students' knowledge about the words used for animal sounds. Help children cut out the two circles. With the smaller circle on top, attach them with a paper fastener. Children can then turn the top wheel to find the sound for each animal. Follow up by choosing several students to tape-record the sounds that different animals make. Then play the tape for the class and have children guess which animals are "talking."

⠿ More Cross-Curricular Activities

MAKE A FARM (Social Studies) The animals in this book live together on a farm. Have children make a classroom farm. Help them create farm animals and buildings—barn, silo, farmhouse—out of modeling clay. Children can put their farm on the top of a table or a counter. If children have small plastic animals or toy trucks, they might add these to the farm, too. Encourage children to label the parts of their farm.

SING, SING A SONG (Music) Have children sing "Old MacDonald Had a Farm." Be sure children include all of the animals mentioned in the book as well as any other farm animals they know.

ACT IT OUT (Dramatic Play) Have the class act out *"Buzz," Said the Bee.* Help children make stick or fabric puppets of the animals. Divide jobs among children, such as puppet maker, scenery designer, actor/puppeteer, and audience members. Allow enough time to practice, then put on the play.

Name That Animal

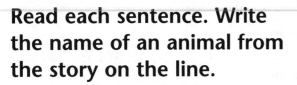

Read each sentence. Write the name of an animal from the story on the line.

| pig | hen |
| sheep | cow |

1. The pig took a bow

and sat on a _____.

2. The hen danced a jig

and sat on a _____.

3. The cow began to weep

and sat on a _____.

4. The duck quacked again

and sat on a _____.

Go back and circle all the words that name animals in each sentence.

THE HELLO READER! ACTIVITY BOOK SCHOLASTIC PROFESSIONAL BOOKS

Name _____

We Speak

Cut out the circles.

Put the small
circle on top.

Use a 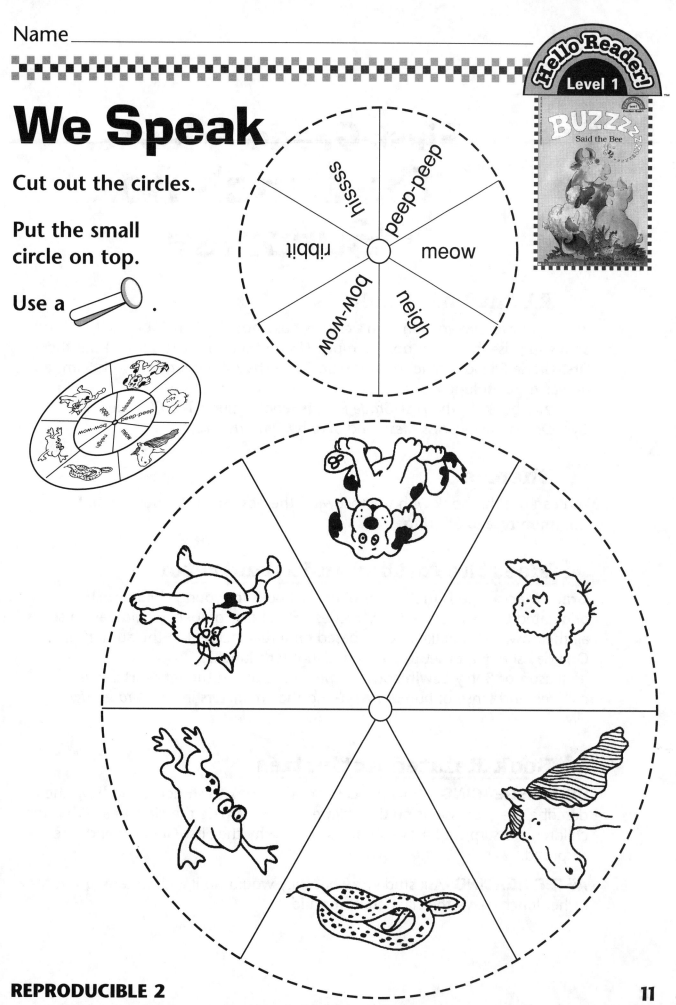.

peep-peep

hissss

ribbit

meow

bow-wow

neigh

First-Grade Friends: The Lunch Box Surprise

▪ About This Book

It's lunchtime. Everyone in Sam's class is busy opening lunch boxes. Much to Sam's surprise, his lunch box is empty. His mother forgot to pack it! But the First-Grade Friends come to his rescue. They share their lunches with Sam, and he has the best lunch ever.

Other books in the *First-Grade Friends* series include *The Classroom Pet, The Gym Day Winner, Recess Mess,* and *Sharing Time Troubles.*

▪ Themes

You can use this book with the following themes: **School, Friendship, Food, Community,** and **Sharing.**

▪ Meet the Author and Illustrator

Grace Maccarone is the author of many books for young children. She originated the *First-Grade Friends* series so that first graders would have a series all their own. This initial book is based on a real incident in the author's life. One day she did forget to pack her daughter's lunch!

Illustrator **Betsy Lewin** adds the perfect touch to the series. Her love of children and sense of humor help bring the characters in *First-Grade Friends* alive.

▪ Book-Related Activities

BEFORE READING Show the cover of this book to students and have them describe the expressions on the children's faces. Guide the class to see that the children are surprised. Have students guess why the First-Grade Friends are surprised.

AFTER READING Ask students what they would do if a classmate forgot his or her lunch. Have the class brainstorm ideas.

◼ Activities for the Reproducibles

SAM IS NOT SAD, SAM IS GLAD (Language Arts) As a literacy-building activity, introduce students to rhyming word families with Reproducible 3. Encourage students to add more words to each column. To extend learning, compile students' responses onto three *Rhyming Word Family* charts: *-ad* words, *-am* words, and *-ot* words. Display the charts around the room for emergent readers and writers to refer to and borrow from. Challenge students to find words that rhyme with these endings: *-at, -ed, -it, -op,* and *-ug.*

MAKE A GIANT SANDWICH (Picture Reading—Sequence) Use Reproducible 4 to review the reading skill of sequence with your students. Provide scissors and glue so students can complete the activity. Tell children to paste the pictures in order on a separate sheet of paper. For fun, students might enjoy making a giant class sandwich. Have each child draw and color a favorite sandwich filling. Draw a slice of bread on the bottom of a long piece of butcher paper. Have children take turns layering their fillings on the bread. At the top, draw another piece of bread. Add a title: *Giant Class Sandwich.*

◼ More Cross-Curricular Activities

WE HAVE FEELINGS (Language Arts) Review some of the feelings that the characters in the book show. Then have students find words in the story that describe feelings: *sad, mad, sorry.* What other words can students think of to describe feelings? Have children choose a word and draw a picture to show that feeling.

SUPER SANDWICHES GRAPH (Math) What's the best sandwich of all? Peanut butter and jelly? Bologna and cheese? Invite each child to record his or her choice on a sheet of paper. Then work together to tally the results and create a bar graph of the top five favorites.

GOOD FOODS TO EAT (Health) Ask children if they think the First-Grade Friends ate healthful lunches. Why or why not? Make a list of healthful foods. Then invite children to cut out pictures from magazines and make a collaborative collage entitled *Good Food That's Good for Us!*

Sam Is Not Sad, Sam Is Glad

Read each word.
Underline the ending.

P<u>am</u>	had	jam
sad	ham	mad
spot	Sam	forgot

Write the word under its ending.
Can you think of other words with these endings?
Write them on the lines.

-ad	-am	-ot
	Pam	

Write a rhyme of your own.

_____

REPRODUCIBLE 3

Name_____

Make a Giant Sandwich

Cut out the pictures.
Paste them in order.

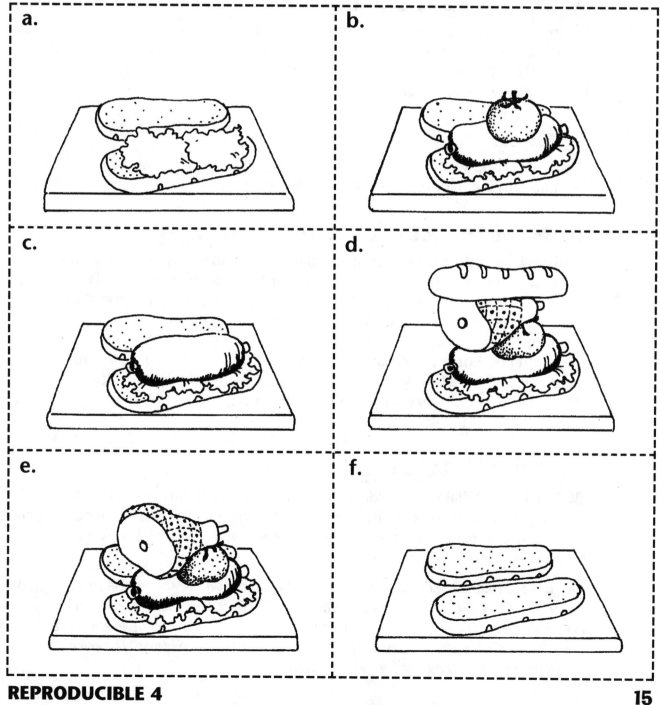

a.

b.

c.

d.

e.

f.

REPRODUCIBLE 4

Hello Reader!
Level 1

Footprints
in the Snow

by Cynthia Benjamin
Illustrated by Jacqueline Rogers

Footprints in the Snow

▣ About This Book

During a winter snowstorm, a rabbit hops, a deer runs, a bear stomps, a beaver swims, a fox races, an owl flies, a squirrel hurries, a mouse scampers, and a child walks—home. All of the creatures in this book find their way home, leaving footprints in the snow.

▣ Themes

This book works well with the following themes: **Winter, Snow, Seasons, Animals, Animal Homes,** and **Forest Animals.**

▣ Meet the Author and Illustrator

Cynthia Benjamin works at home writing educational materials for young children. When Benjamin sent her manuscript for *Footprints in the Snow* to Scholastic, the editors of the *Hello Reader!* series recognized that the story would make a perfect nonfiction selection since it was easy-to-read and scientifically accurate.

Jacqueline Rogers, well-known for her beautiful renderings of animals and people, was the perfect illustrator for the story. Rogers is also the illustrator of these *Hello Reader!* books: *Monkey See, Monkey Do; Once Upon a Springtime;* and *We Eat Dinner in the Bathtub.*

▣ Book-Related Activities

BEFORE READING Ask children to tell you what footprints are. Have them find the footprints on the cover of this book. Ask: In what other places can footprints be left? *(sand, dirt, mud, cement)* Have children guess what other creatures will be leaving footprints in this book.

AFTER READING Review with children the places where the animals in the book live. *(The rabbit lives in a warren underground. The deer seek shelter under the evergreen trees. The bear carves out a cave. The beavers build a lodge in the water. The foxes live underground. The owl and squirrels live in nests in the trees. The mice stay warm under twigs. The child lives in a house.)*

▓ Activities for the Reproducibles

FOLLOW THE FOOTPRINTS (Following Directions) Reproducible 5 is a good tool to use when reinforcing children's ability to follow directions. Make sure children have a black crayon, a red crayon, and a green crayon.

WHOSE FOOTPRINTS ARE THESE? (Picture Reading)
Reproducible 6 extends children's knowledge of animals. Model for children how to cut out and assemble the picture strips. Students may need help cutting out the window slits. Demonstrate how to slide the pictures through the windows to match an animal with its footprint. Help children look for identifying characteristics on each animal's feet to help them make their matches.

▓ More Cross-Curricular Activities

ON THE MOVE (Language Arts) Review the verbs in this book. Can children name other action words that describe how animals move? Keep a list of students' answers. Then have each child choose an animal and a verb from the list. On a blank sheet of paper, have each child write a sentence using the same format as the sentences in the book. When children are finished, collect their papers and staple them together into a book titled *On the Move*. Put this book on display in the classroom or have children take turns taking it home to share with their families.

WHERE WE LIVE (Social Studies) Tell children that the animals in this book are forest animals. Have children work together to create a forest diorama showing the kinds of homes forest animals live in. Children can use the book as a reference. Provide students with one large box or individual shoe boxes, absorbent cotton to use as the snow, construction paper, pieces of fabric, glue, and scissors. If children want, they can draw or cut out pictures of forest animals from magazines to use in this diorama. Encourage children to write sentences on index cards that describe the homes of these animals.

A SCAVENGER FOOT HUNT (Creative Play) Divide the class into two groups. One group of students will design a scavenger hunt. Have these children trace their footprints on butcher paper and cut them out, making enough footprints to get from one spot to another. Then give each child in this group a crayon. Tell children to color in all of their footprints with their crayon. Now have children tape their paper footprints to the floor, leading to a place or thing on the scavenger hunt. Children should write clues and place them at the beginning of their footprint trail. Then have the children in the second group go on the scavenger hunt, following the footprints around the classroom.

Follow the Footprints

With a black crayon, draw a line that follows the rabbit's footprints.

With a red crayon, draw a line that follows the bear's footprints.

With a green crayon, draw a line that follows the boy's footprints.

Hello Reader!

Level 1

Footprints in the Snow

by Cynthia Benjamin
Illustrated by Jacqueline Rogers

REPRODUCIBLE 5

Whose Footprints Are These?

Cut out the strips.
Slip one strip through
the top slits.
Slip one strip through
the bottom slits.
Move the strips to match
each animal with its tracks.

Here Comes the Snow

About This Book

The children bundle up in their winter clothes. They go outside. They wait and wait. No snow. Finally they see one flake, two flakes. Here comes the snow! What fun—the children ride their sled, make snow angels, have a snowball fight, build a snowman, and, of course, drink hot cocoa when they go indoors!

Themes

This book works well with the following themes: **Winter, Seasons, Weather, Families,** and **Friendship.**

Meet the Author and Illustrator

Angela Shelf Medearis has written many books for young children. She likes to base most of them on experiences from her own childhood. Her energy and sense of fun come across in her writing.

The delightful art style of **Maxie Chambliss** complements the story and helps young readers visualize the action. Maxie Chambliss is well-known for her lively children's book illustrations.

Book-Related Activities

BEFORE READING Ask children if they have ever seen snow. Do they like it? (For those students who have not experienced snow, ask if anyone has ever described it to them. Do they think they would like snow?) Display the book cover. Do students think the children on the cover like snow? Have students give reasons for their answers. *(The title of the book is* Here Comes the Snow; *the children and the dog all have big smiles on their faces. They look as if they are enjoying their sled ride.)*

AFTER READING Have children brainstorm a list of words that they associate with the word *snow.* *(Accept words such as:* white, icy, cold, wet, slippery, mittens, jackets, boots, hats, scarves, sleds, skis, snowboards, snowballs, snowman, falling, running, jumping.) Write these words on the chalkboard. Then have children draw or cut out pictures from magazines that illustrate these words. Compile children's pictures and words into a classroom collage titled *Here Comes the Snow.*

Activities for the Reproducibles

BRRR, IT'S COLD (Language Arts) While working on Reproducible 7, children use critical-thinking skills to compare clothes worn in the winter to those worn in the summer. Ask children why they think people dress differently for different types of weather. *(Accept such answers as: to protect themselves from getting sick; for comfort; to protect themselves from high or low temperatures, hail, wind, too much sun.)*

BUILD A SNOWPERSON (Art) Encourage children to be creative as they work on Reproducible 8. They can use the pictures on the page and draw the features on their snowperson, or glue on pieces of fabric, buttons, glitter, or ribbon that you provide. Have crayons, paints, scissors, and glue available. Suggest that children cut out their finished snowpeople and mount them on cardboard. (You might precut these cardboard forms. Children can paste their snowpeople directly onto them.) Help children punch a hole at the top of their snowperson and tie yarn through the hole. Children can use them as ornaments.

More Cross-Curricular Activities

READ ALL ABOUT IT! (Reading—Comparing and Contrasting) Suggest that children take turns reading these books about snow—*The Jacket I Wear in the Snow* by Shirley Neitzel (Greenwillow) and *The Snowy Day* by Ezra Jack Keats (Puffin Books). Have children compare these books to *Here Comes the Snow*. Ask them: Did the characters in the books dress the same way? Did they play the same games? Did they have to wait for the snow to fall? As children answer these questions, make a comparison chart to help them easily compare the books. Post this chart on a classroom bulletin board.

WE READ ABOUT SNOW			
TITLE	Here Comes the Snow	The Snowy Day	The Jacket I Wear in the Snow
SNOW	waited for the snow to come	snow fell during the night	
CLOTHING	wore coats, boots, mittens, scarves	wore snowsuit	wore jacket, scarf, hat, mittens, jeans, sweater, boots, long underwear, socks
ACTIVITY	made snow angels; had a snowball fight; built a snowman	made tracks in the snow; made snow angels; pretended to be a mountain climber	tried to ride a sled
ENDING	drank hot cocoa	took a warm bath; next day snow falls; go outside again	went indoors; got undressed; had cocoa, doughnuts, cupcakes

HOW FAST DOES IT MELT? (Science) Have children predict how long it would take for an ice cube to melt indoors. Record students' predictions on a chart. Then conduct an experiment to test their predictions by placing an ice cube in a tin foil pan. How many guesses came close? Have children discuss ways they think they could make the ice cube melt even faster. *(place the tray in the direct sunlight, put the tray on a radiator, put the tray on a lit stove or inside a hot oven)*

Name_____

Brrr, It's Cold

Look at these pictures.
Color the things you wear in the snow.

Here Comes the SNOW

by Angela Shelf Medearis
Illustrated by Maxie Chambliss

Use the words in the word box.
Write the word under the correct picture.

| boots | mittens |
| coat | scarf |

What do you wear on
your head when it snows?
Draw a picture here.

REPRODUCIBLE 7

Name _____

Build a Snowperson

You can build a snowperson.
Cut out and paste the pictures
on another page.

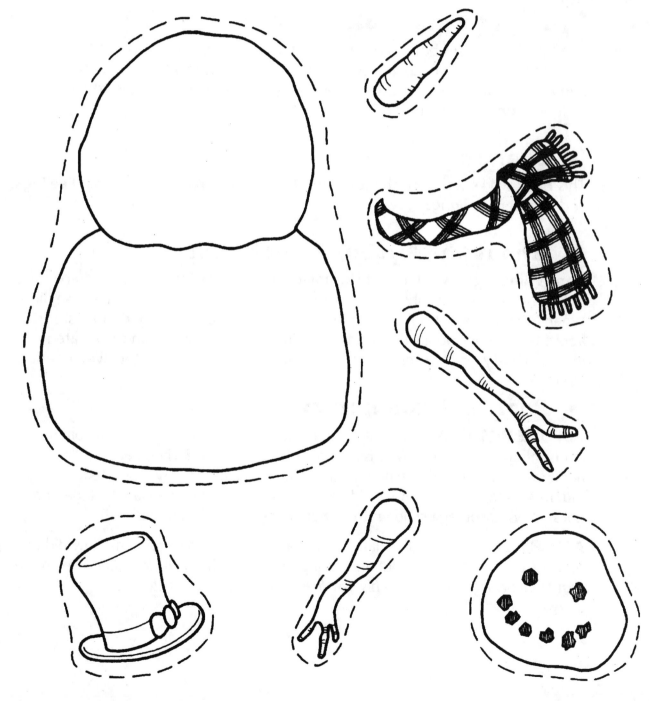

THE HELLO READER! ACTIVITY BOOK SCHOLASTIC PROFESSIONAL BOOKS

I Hate My Bow!

■ About This Book

The little dog in this book is having a very bad day. He hates everything. Suddenly, he has an idea, and with the help of some new friends, he turns his bad day into a good one. Other *Hello Reader!* books featuring this little dog include *I Am Lost!* and *Don't Cut My Hair!*

■ Themes

This book works well with the following themes: **Animals, Pets, Dogs, Feelings,** and **Problem Solving.**

■ About the Author-Illustrator

Hans Wilhelm has written and illustrated many books for young children. Because of his delightful sense of humor, his books keep young readers smiling. When Wilhelm saw this little dog in real life, he couldn't help writing a story about him. Other books that Hans Wilhelm has both written and illustrated include *I'll Always Love You, The Royal Raven,* and the books in the *Tyrone* series.

■ Book-Related Activities

BEFORE READING Have children look at the book cover as you or a volunteer reads the title aloud. Ask: Who is saying, "I hate my bow"? Then have children name words that could describe the little dog's feelings. (angry, disgusted, mad, sad, frustrated, unhappy) Ask children if they have ever felt the way the little dog does. Why? Encourage children to identify things they like and dislike.

AFTER READING Ask the class: What was the little dog's problem? How did he solve it? Do you think his solution was a good one? Why? *(Children should recognize that the little dog had fun with his new friends at the end of the story.)*

▚ Activities for the Reproducibles

GOOD IDEAS (Social Studies) Reproducible 9 helps children focus on problem solving. It also provides a way to review the story. As you hand out the reproducible, remind students that the little dog had problems with several things. Provide children with crayons and have them draw pictures to show the dog's solution to three things he didn't like. Follow up with a discussion on how students would solve similar problems, such as not wanting to wear something. Encourage students to share their problem-solving strategies.

SAME DOG, NEW STORY (Language Arts—Writing) Reproducible 10 sets up repetitive frames from the story and allows children to rewrite the story using new words. Encourage children to "think like the little dog would think." To extend this activity, have children share their ideas. If you like, have the class flesh out one of the stories and write it as a class book. Assign different parts to children to work on. Have children take turns reading the completed book aloud.

▚ More Cross Curricular Activities

GIVE THE DOG A NAME (Creative Thinking) The dog in the book does not have a name. Have children suggest names that they think would fit. List the names on the chalkboard. Then take a vote. Of course, the name that gets the most votes, wins.

DOGS, DOGS, AND MORE DOGS (Classifying) Have children bring in pictures of their pet dogs, or cut out pictures from magazines of different dogs. Help children identify the types of dogs. Mount each child's picture on a piece of oak tag and write the type of dog below the picture. Then have children classify these dogs—small, large, short-haired, long-haired, ears pointing up, floppy ears, etc. Do children know what the type of dog in the book is? *(Maltese)*

Name_____

Good Ideas

The little dog has problems.
Draw a picture to show what he
does about each problem.

The dog hates...	What he does...

REPRODUCIBLE 9

Hello Reader!
Level 1

Same Dog, New Story

Change the story you just read.
Fill in the blank lines with a new idea.

I hate my _____.

I have an idea. I will _____

_____

_____.

I love my _____

_____.

I'm a Seed

About This Book

In this *Hello Science Reader!* book, Jean Marzollo compares the two seeds growing side by side and shows how they are alike and how they are different. One seed turns into a marigold plant and the other, a pumpkin plant. Readers follow the step-by-step growth of these two seeds. Other books in this series are: *I Am Water, I Am Fire, I'm a Caterpillar, I Am an Apple,* and *I'm a Rock.*

Themes

This book works well with the following themes: **Growth, Plants,** and **Spring**.

Meet the Author and Illustrator

Jean Marzollo is a highly acclaimed children's book author who writes the riddles in the best-selling series of *I Spy* books. Among her other books are *In 1492; In 1776; Ten Cats Have Hats; Happy Birthday, Martin Luther King;* and *Valentine Cats.* Marzollo loves to write all kinds of books from poetry to easy-to-read and early chapter books to nonfiction.

    Judith Moffatt always thought she would become a watercolor painter, but she became interested in paper collage while helping her sister create a calendar. Moffatt became enamored of the feeling of the scissors gliding across paper. She has illustrated several books with her cut-paper technique, including *Too Many Rabbits; Crocodile! Crocodile! Stories Told Around the World;* and *Snakes!*

Book-Related Activities

BEFORE READING Ask children to tell you what they think a seed is. Then show them the cover of the book. Have a volunteer point out the two seeds on the cover. Ask: What do you think the girl is going to do with her seeds? How do you know?

AFTER READING In the book, one seed grows into a marigold plant and the other, a pumpkin plant. Have children brainstorm names of flowers, fruits, and vegetables. Write their suggestions on chart paper, divided into three columns—*Flowers, Fruits, Vegetables.* Children can draw the items listed and paste them under the correct headings.

✖ Activities for the Reproducibles

FROM SEED TO FLOWER (Reading in the Content Area—Science)
Reproducible 11 helps children review some of the scientific words they have learned in the book. Be sure each child has scissors, paste, and crayons. Choose volunteers to read the sentences on the reproducible or read them aloud to the class. Help students identify the flower. *(pansy)* When students are finished, collect their papers and display them in the science corner.

HERE WE GROW (Science) Reproducible 12 helps children extend their knowledge of seeds. Before children start, review these facts:

- plants have many parts—roots, stems, leaves, flowers, seeds
- some plants grow above the soil and others grow below the soil
- most plants have green leaves
- all plants need sun, water, air, and nutrients to grow
- seeds grow into plants that produce flowers, fruits, or vegetables

You might transfer these facts onto a chart titled *How Plants Are the Same and Different*. Children can help by drawing or cutting out pictures to illustrate these facts. Post this chart on a classroom bulletin board. As children learn new facts, these can be added to the chart.

✖ More Cross-Curricular Activities

MAKE A SPONGE GARDEN (Science) To make a sponge garden, gather different kinds of small seeds. (Grass seed works well.) Give each child a small piece of sponge, a paper cup, and some seeds. Tell them what kind of seeds they have. Have children soak the sponge thoroughly, place it in the cup, and add more water. Tell children that there should always be water in the cup so that the sponge does not dry out. Then have children sprinkle their seeds on top of the sponge. Have them label their sponge plants. When leaves appear, add liquid plant food to the water to supply nutrients. Line up the sponge plants along a windowsill.

HOW MANY SEEDS ARE IN A ... ? (Math) Bring several different fruits and vegetables to class. Hold up each item and ask children to predict how many seeds each one contains. Write each child's prediction next to his or her name on a chart. Next, cut each fruit or vegetable and have children examine and count the seeds. Record the actual number on the chart. Dry the seeds and add some to the chart. Plant the rest of the seeds and see which grow.

ABOVE AND BELOW IN THE GARDEN (Art) Divide a long sheet of mural paper horizontally. Draw a soil line to suggest "above the ground" and "below the ground." Have children brainstorm what they might see in these two areas. Provide materials such as pieces of fabric and/or construction paper, scissors, glue, and paste. Ask children to create their own garden, filling in these two areas accurately.

Name _____

From Seed to Flower

Read the sentence in each box.

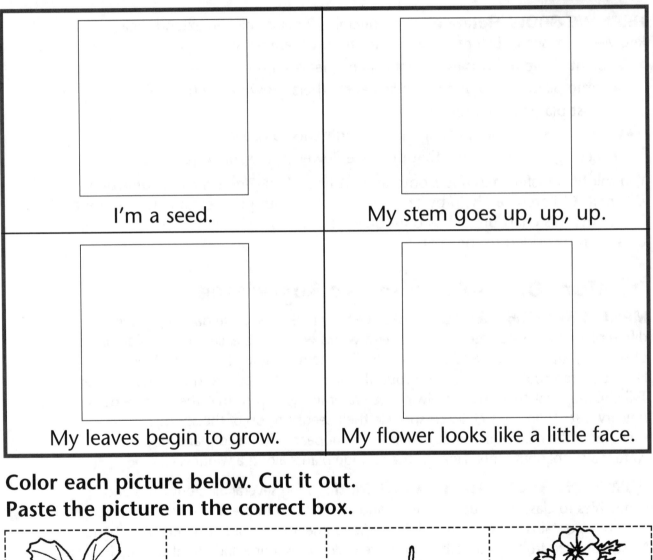

I'm a seed.	My stem goes up, up, up.
My leaves begin to grow.	My flower looks like a little face.

Color each picture below. Cut it out.
Paste the picture in the correct box.

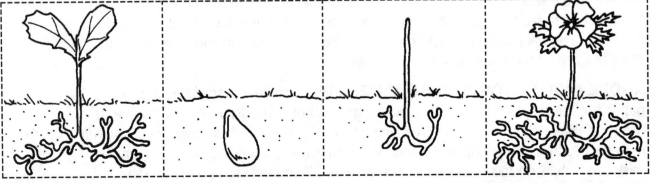

REPRODUCIBLE 11

Name ____________________

Hello Reader! Level 1

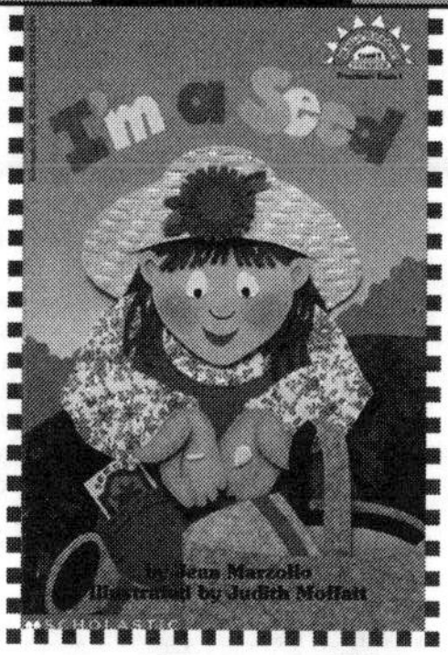

Here We Grow

Fill in the blank lines. Use the words in the word box. You will use some words more than once.

above	green
flower	good
sun	below
pretty	vegetable

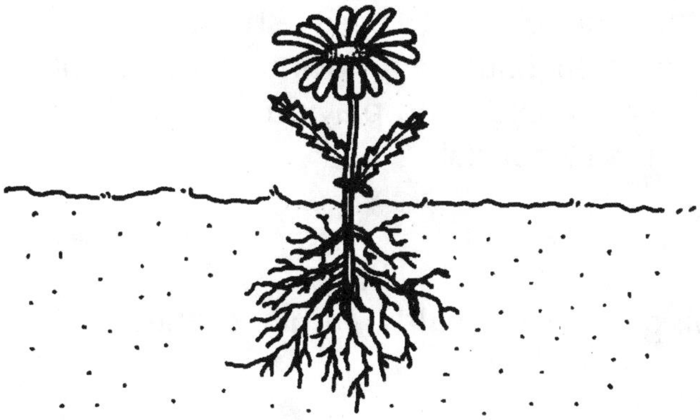

I am a daisy.

1. I have ______________ leaves.
2. I grow ______________ the ground.
3. I need water and ______________ to grow.
4. I am a ______________.
5. I am ______________ to look at.

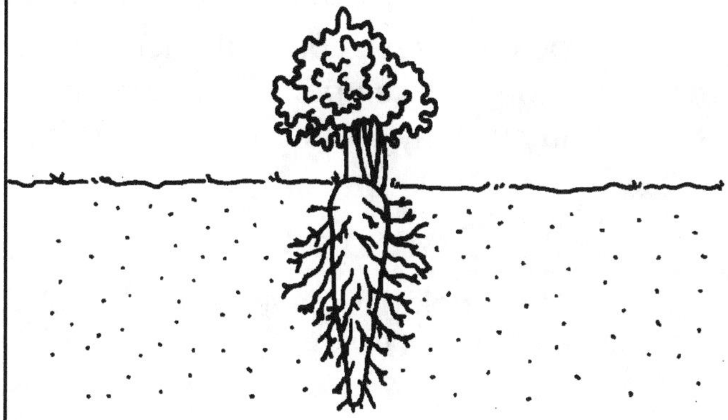

I am a carrot.

1. I have ______________ leaves.
2. I grow ______________ the ground.
3. I also need water and ______________ to grow.
4. I am a ______________.
5. I am ______________ to eat.

Itchy, Itchy Chicken Pox

About This Book

One spot. Then more! Uh-oh! A boy has chicken pox! Those itchy, itchy chicken pox just keep coming! There's lotion, oatmeal baths, and loving care. But still more chicken pox. There's resting, reading, eating, and playing. Finally, those itchy, itchy spots go away, and life returns to normal.

Themes

This book ties in well with the following themes: **Health**, **Families**, and **Growing Up**.

Meet the Author and Illustrator

When **Grace Maccarone**'s daughter was a toddler, she came in contact with chicken pox. Although she didn't get chicken pox then, the author (and concerned mother) questioned doctors and read many books on the subject. Throughout her research, she could not get the phrase, "itchy, itchy chicken pox" out of her mind. So, she wrote a story using the phrase. *Itchy, Itchy Chicken Pox* was published two years after she wrote the story, the same spring that Grace Maccarone's daughter *did* come down with chicken pox!

Betsy Lewin's illustrations help give readers a good picture of this "itchy, twitchy" experience.

Book-Related Activities

BEFORE READING Ask children if they have ever had chicken pox or another disease. Can they describe what it felt like? What were some of the things their families did for them while they were sick?

AFTER READING Remind children that someone who is sick needs care. What advice would students give to a classmate who doesn't feel well? *(tell the teacher, see the school nurse, lie down, call parents)* Children might also make a list of good rules to follow when they are sick. *(take your medicine, get plenty of rest, drink water)*

▞ Activities for the Reproducibles

THEY COME AND THEY GO (Reading—Order of Events) As children read the book, they discover the progression chicken pox takes—from the first few spots to total body coverage to recovery. Reproducible 13 helps children understand this order of events in the story. Have children cut out the faces and paste them next to the appropriate lines from the story. You may want to read the lines aloud as children work.

GET WELL SOON (Art) Children can make the simple finger puppet on Reproducible 14 as a get-well gift. Provide crayons for children to color their puppets. Remind students that the two circles are for their fingers. You may need to help some children cut out these holes. For stronger puppets, have children paste their puppets on oak tag or index cards. Students can also use the puppets to talk about things that cheer them up when they are sick.

▞ More Cross-Curricular Activities

MY GOOD HEALTH CHART (Math) Have children make a health habit chart. Across the top, they can write the days of the week. Down the left side, they can write reminders such as: Got lots of sleep; Brushed my teeth; Took a bath. Children can check off the activities they do each day.

READ AND REST (Language Arts) Reading (or being read to) is a good activity for a bedridden child. Invite students to compile a list of favorite books that a sick classmate might enjoy. As children name a book, have them tell why they are recommending it. You might send this list home to families.

WE HELP OTHERS (Social Studies) Have children talk about the things they have done to help someone who was sick. Trace and cut out hand shapes from construction paper. Write one helpful idea that children suggest on each hand *(made get-well card, lent book)* and paste it onto a large poster titled *Helping Hands*. Display the poster in the classroom to remind children that they can be helpers.

Name _____

They Come and They Go

Cut out the faces. Paste a face next
to the sentence it tells about.

1. Daddy counts my itchy spots.
   Lots and lots of chicken pox.

2. And then...no new spots. Hooray!
   I'm okay! I can go to school today!

3. A spot. A spot. Another spot.
   Uh-oh! Chicken pox!

Draw a face that shows how you feel when you first get sick.	Draw a face that shows how you feel when you are well again.

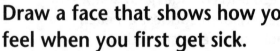

beginning   middle   end

34

REPRODUCIBLE 13

Name_____

Get Well Soon

Draw a funny puppet.
Cut out your puppet.

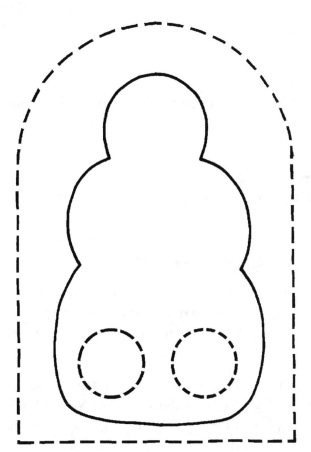

This is how you
use your puppet.

✄ **Give your puppet to a friend who is sick.**

My Tooth Is About to Fall Out

About This Book

A young girl describes what happens before and after her tooth falls out. This book is a great addition to your classroom library during National Dental Health Month in February.

Themes

This book works well with the following themes: **All About Me**, **Health**, **Dental Health**, and **Growing Up.**

Author Notes

Grace Maccarone wrote this book for her daughter to celebrate the loss of her first tooth.

Book-Related Activities

BEFORE READING Ask children to raise a hand if they have lost a tooth. Has anybody lost more than one tooth? How many children are missing teeth now? Have children describe what it feels like when a tooth is loose. Jot down these words on the chalkboard.

AFTER READING What words did the girl in the story use to describe her loose tooth? Compare these to the words students used. What new facts about baby teeth did students learn? *(They have 20. Big teeth grow underneath. Roots of baby teeth dissolve and shrink until teeth get loose and fall out.)*

Activities for the Reproducibles

"ALL" IN THE FAMILY (Language Arts) Reproducible 15 is a literacy-building activity. If you want, children can work together in small groups to think of words that end in *-all*. When children are finished, compile their list of *-all* words on a chart and display it in the classroom. Then have children write two rhyming sentences that end in *-all* words. Follow up by asking children to find other rhyming words in the poem. (think, shrink)

MY TEETH FALL OUT (**Health**) Reproducible 16 allows children to learn more about themselves. Be sure children have crayons or markers and small mirrors. Have children use the mirrors to look inside their mouths. Do they see the same teeth in their mouths as on the reproducible? If children are having difficulty, help them find the teeth they are missing and put an X on the reproducible. To extend this activity, make a bar graph of how many teeth each child in your class has lost. This chart could be ongoing throughout the year. As a child loses a tooth, record it on the graph. Every few months, ask questions about the graph: Who has lost the most teeth? Who has lost the fewest? Is there anyone who hasn't lost a tooth yet?

More Cross-Curricular Activities

BRUSH UP, BRUSH DOWN, BRUSH ALL AROUND (**Health**) Make a classroom chart showing children the correct way to brush their teeth. Place these steps on the chart. You might choose children to illustrate each step.

Step 1: Brush the outside of your teeth—up and down.

Step 2: Brush the inside of your teeth—up and down.

Step 3: Brush the teeth in the back of your mouth—back and forth.

Step 4: Brush your teeth at the gumline.

Ask children: What else can you do to take care of your teeth? *(brush often, visit your dentist regularly, eat foods rich in calcium)*

STRONG TEETH (**Science**) This experiment shows children how the acid from the germs in their mouth can dissolve the calcium in their teeth and weaken them.

You will need: white vinegar, plain water, two pieces of eggshell, two cups

1. Put one piece of eggshell in a cup.
2. Cover this eggshell with a few tablespoons of vinegar.
3. Put the other piece of eggshell in the second cup.
4. Cover this piece with a few tablespoons of plain water.
5. Soak the shells for a few days. Then have children feel them. Ask: Which one is still hard? Which one is soft and weak?
6. Put the soft eggshell back in the cup with the vinegar. Leave it until all the vinegar evaporates. Then have children look at it. Ask: Is there a white powder at the bottom of the cup? What do you think this is? *[The white powder is calcium. The calcium was removed from the eggshell (the teeth) by the vinegar (the tooth-germ acid).]*

Name_____

"All" in the Family

Read these sentences. Find three words that rhyme with *all*. Write them on the web.

My Loose Tooth

I hope it doesn't fall
while I am playing ball.

I hope it doesn't fall
into my meatball
or in my spaghetti.

My roots, I think,
dissolve and shrink
until they're small.

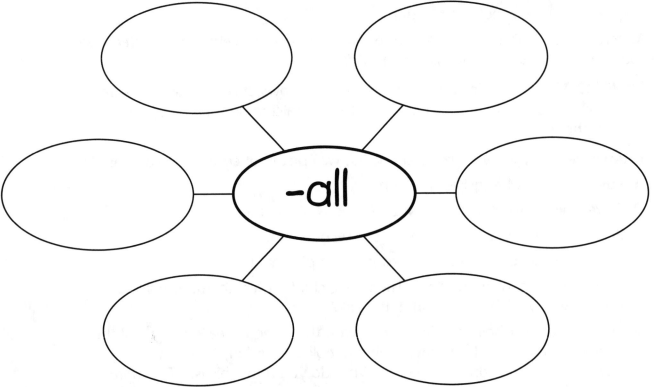

-all

■ **Think of three more -*all* words.**
Add them to the web.

38

Name _____

My Teeth Fall Out

Here's a picture of a mouth.
Put an X on any teeth you have lost.

I have lost _____ teeth.

Willie's Wonderful Pet

About This Book

It's Pet Day at school. Al brings his dog, Cathy has a cat, Henry has a rabbit, George has a goldfish, Rita has a bird, Mike has a hamster, and Willie has a worm. The children in Willie's class don't think a worm is a real pet because it can't do anything, so they tease Willie. But, much to their surprise, Willie's pet does more than anyone can imagine—he gets things started.

Themes

You can use this book when teaching the following themes: **Pets, Animals, School,** and **Friendship.**

Meet the Author and Illustrator

Mel Cebulash wrote this story in 1972 for Scholastic Book Services. At that time, Cebulash worked as an editorial director at Scholastic. When the *Hello Reader!* editors read this book, they decided to reissue it as part of the series.

　　The new illustrations were done by well-known artist **George Ford.** Ford is also the illustrator of *Ray Charles* (a Coretta Scott King Award winning book), the *What-a-Baby* board book series, *The Story of Ruby Bridges,* and the *Hello Readers!* books, *Wild, Wild Hair* and *Hanging Out With Mom.*

Book-Related Activities

BEFORE READING Ask children to name animals that can be pets. Then read the title of the book aloud and have children guess what kind of animal Willie's pet might be.

AFTER READING Were children surprised that Willie's pet was a worm? Ask: Who thinks that a worm is a good pet? Why or why not? Encourage children to share their ideas of what makes a good pet. Jot down children's thoughts on the chalkboard. Does everyone in the class agree with each of the items on the list? Why or why not?

✖ Activities for the Reproducibles

WE CAN DO IT (Language Arts) Reproducible 17 helps children review action words. Model how to cut out and staple together the pages of the flip and match book. Be sure to separate each page along the dotted line. Children can then flip the pages to match an animal with a verb from the story. When students finish working, ask them to name other animals and tell what these animals can do. Or choose several children to act out the action words.

HOME SWEET HOME (Social Studies) Reproducible 18 helps children understand one of life's basic necessities—shelter. Discuss the pet homes shown on the reproducible. Ask: Are these the only homes these pets could live in? Why?

   If you have a class pet, discuss with children how to take care of it. If you don't already have a chart describing the care of the pet, this might be a good time to make one and post it next to the pet's home. If you don't have a class pet, ask children to vote on what animal would make a good class pet. Why?

✖ More Cross-Curricular Activities

PETS ON PARADE (Role Playing) Divide the class in half. Tell one group that they will be the pet owners, and the other group will be the judges. Have the owners cut out pictures of pets and mount them on cardboard. Then have them attach their cardboard pets to long dowels. While the owners are doing this, have the judges agree what categories they will present awards for: cutest, ugliest, biggest, smallest, furriest, etc. Have the judges make blue ribbons to hand out. When everyone is ready, have the owners parade their pets in front of the judges. Ask them to tell something special about their pet. Then have the judges vote and hand out the awards.

POPULAR PETS (Math) Ask children to name the kinds of pets they have at home or the kinds they would like to have. Keep a tally on the chalkboard. Then make a bar graph titled *Popular Pets* to show the outcome of the survey. What is the class's favorite pet? Are there any unusual pets listed?

TAKE GOOD CARE OF MY PET (Language Arts—Writing) Have children pretend that they are leaving their pet with a friend or relative while they go on a short vacation. Tell children to write a list of things that the pet-sitter will have to do to take care of the pet. Share children's lists. Have children discuss their ideas. Ask: Do different pets require different things? Why or why not?

Name_____

Hello Reader!
Level 1

Willie's
Wonderful
Pet
by Mel Cebulash
Illustrated by George Ford

We Can Do It

Cut out the pages. Make a flip book.
Match each animal to the page that
shows what it does in the story.

A worm	can sing.	
A cat	can hop.	A rabbit	can jump.
A dog	can run around.	A goldfish	can bark.
A hamster	can crawl.	A bird	can swim in a bowl.

THE HELLO READER! ACTIVITY BOOK   SCHOLASTIC PROFESSIONAL BOOKS

REPRODUCIBLE 17

Name_____

Home Sweet Home

Cut out the pictures below.
Paste each animal in its home.
Then color the animal and its home.

Willie's
Wonderful
Pet
by Mel Cebulash
Illustrated by George Ford

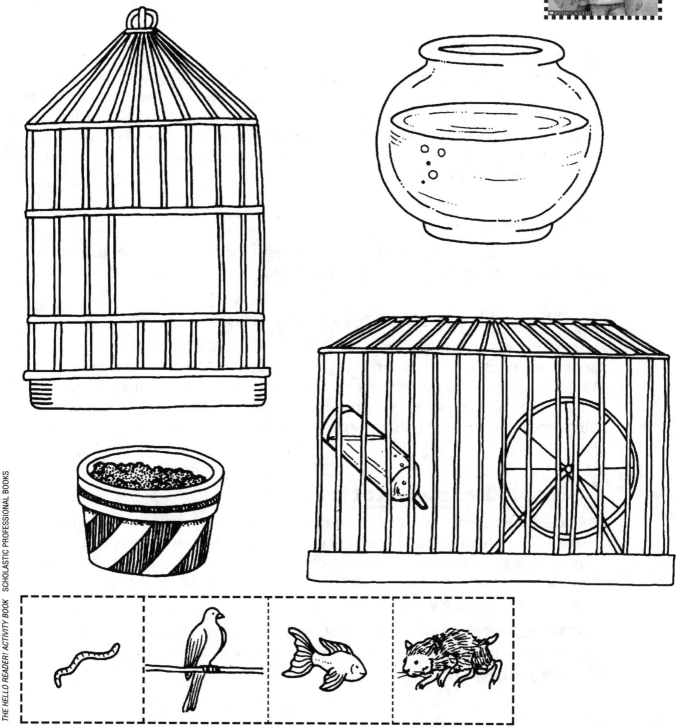

THE HELLO READER! ACTIVITY BOOK   SCHOLASTIC PROFESSIONAL BOOKS

The Cows Are in the Corn

About This Book

All of the animals on this farm are in places they shouldn't be, and they won't come out. The cows are in the corn; the pigs are in the figs; the goats are in the oats; the rams are in the yams; and the bees are in the peas. Brother, Sister, Uncle, Auntie, and Father each try to shout them out. But they can't. So they call Mother, who doesn't shout but does bang and clang a big ladle on a pot and rousts them out.

Themes

This book works well with the following themes: **Farm Animals, Food, Humor, Families, Communities,** and **Problem Solving.**

Meet the Author-Illustrator

James Young sent a rough draft of this book to Edie Weinberg, Cartwheel Books' art director. She was very enthusiastic about it and showed it to Grace Maccarone. Mr. Young works very quickly and requires little editing, so the editors were able to produce the book in record time. James Young's other books include *Everyone Loves the Moon, Old Mrs. Mopiter,* and *Penelope and the Pirates.*

Book-Related Activities

BEFORE READING Ask children to name some animals that live on a farm. Make a list of these animals. Then ask children to name some foods that are grown on a farm. Keep a separate list of these foods. Based on the title, have children guess what they think this book will be about. Ask: Will it be a silly or a serious story? Why do you think so?

AFTER READING Have children look back at the lists of animals and foods to determine which items the author used. Then have children tell why they thought the book was silly or serious.

Activities for the Reproducibles

SOME SILLY RHYMES (Language Arts) Reproducible 19 allows children to work with rhyming words in a fun way. Choose volunteers to read the sentences and the words in the box aloud to the class. Remind children that these sentences are supposed to be silly. When children finish working on the reproducible, have them choose a sentence and write and illustrate it on a separate sheet of paper. Hang children's artwork in the classroom. Let students who would like to make more silly sentences fill in the blanks in these sentences:

The lamb is in the _____. *(jam)*

The ants are in the _____. *(plants)*

The spider is in the _____. *(cider)*

The raccoons are in the _____. *(prunes)*

The toucans are in the _____. *(pecans)*

SET THE SCENE (Art) Reproducible 20 provides a hands-on activity that helps children re-create the story. Assign children to work in groups of five. Help them cut out the farm animals. Then pass out drawing paper and crayons. Have children fold the paper in half. Explain that one half is the ground, and the other half is a farm crop. Have each child in a group draw one crop—corn, figs, oats, yams, or peas—on one side of their paper. After coloring the animal that eats this crop in the story, children can paste the animal on the ground side of the paper so that the crop provides a background. Each group can then retell the story using the dioramas.

More Cross-Curricular Activities

LIFE ON A FARM (Social Studies) Have children draw or cut out pictures from magazines that show the kinds of foods grown on a farm as well as pictures of animals that live on a farm. Remind children that there are many kinds of farms—fruit farms, dairy farms, vegetable farms, ranches. Have children work together using a long sheet of butcher paper to make a mural of life on a farm. For their mural, children can choose one kind of farm or include foods and animals from different farms. When children finish, hang the mural on a wall of the classroom. Give it the title *Life on a Farm*.

ROLLICKING GOOD FUN (Creative Dramatics) This book is especially good fun for children to act out since they can shout. Choose several students to play the different roles. Other children can choral read the part of the narrator. You might give the child who has the role of Mother a ladle and a pot or bucket so children can hear what the animals in the book heard.

Name_____

Some Silly Rhymes

Read each sentence.
Underline the name of the animal.
Choose a food from the box that
rhymes with the animal.
Write the word on the
blank line.

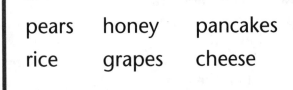

pears	honey	pancakes
rice	grapes	cheese

1. The apes are in the _____.

2. The bears are in the _____.

3. The snakes are in the _____.

4. The mice are in the _____.

5. The bunny is in the _____.

6. The fleas are in the _____.

46

REPRODUCIBLE 19

Name_____

Set the Scene

Cut out the animals.
Use them to retell the story.

THE HELLO READER! ACTIVITY BOOK   SCHOLASTIC PROFESSIONAL BOOKS

Fraidy Cats

About This Book

The Fraidy Cats, Sorry and Scamper, can't sleep. Their imaginations are running wild as they envision that the night noises they hear are those of a large dog, a giant snake, a fierce eagle, a dangerous wolf, a wild elephant, and the biggest dinosaur that ever lived, the ultrasaurus. Luckily, the Fraidy Cats remember that the ultrasaurus eats only plants—never cats. So Sorry and Scamper finally fall asleep, certain that the ultrasuarus will stay in their garden and protect them.

Themes

This book ties in well with the following themes: **Humor, Animals, Real and Make-Believe, Imagination,** and **All About Me.**

Meet the Author and Illustrator

Stephen Krensky is the author of many books for young readers. His easy-to-read stories please children because they are often very funny. When he sent in the manuscript for *Fraidy Cats*, his suggestions for the art were just as important as the text itself. He had to think visually for this book in order to make it work.

When **Betsy Lewin** read the manuscript, she was able to interpret Krensky's ideas with her watercolor illustrations. To help children understand this book, the imagined scenes are in a different style from the realistic ones.

Book-Related Activities

BEFORE READING What are the cats on the cover ready to do? Why do children think the cats might be frightened? Have children name some things the Fraidy Cats might fear. Ask children to name things they fear at night. Keep a running list of children's ideas.

AFTER READING Ask children if they thought this book was funny. Have children cite humorous examples from the story. Ask: Why do you think the author called this book *Fraidy Cats*? Why did he choose two cats as the main characters? Review the list of children's night fears. Ask: Were the Fraidy Cats afraid of any of the same things? Why or why not?

⊠ Activities for the Reproducibles

DO YOU REMEMBER? (Reading—Understanding Details in a Story)
Reproducible 21 helps children review the details in the story. It also offers an opportunity to discuss the difference between real and make-believe. Provide scissors and glue so that children can complete the page. Remind children that many of the details occur in the illustrations. If children need help, tell them to look back at the book. To extend this activity, ask children to share their ideas about other sounds they hear at night. What makes the sound? What animal might it remind children of? Save students' ideas.

BAD NIGHT, GOOD NIGHT (Reading—Opposites) Review what an opposite is before passing out Reproducible 22. You may want to use examples from the story pointing out that whenever one cat hears a scary "animal," the other cat hopes the animal will be just the opposite. Have children work with partners to complete the page.

⊠ More Cross-Curricular Activities

FRAIDY CATS CONTINUED (Language Arts—Creative Writing) Have children work in small groups to add another scene to this book. Tell children they can use one of the ideas they discussed previously (see extended activity in the Do You Remember? reproducible section), or they can think about an animal that sounds like one of these:
- a garbage can that falls over
- a balloon that pops
- the cracking of a branch when someone steps on it.

Children can dictate their scenes or write them on paper. Suggest that students illustrate their scenes and share them with each other.

ANIMAL SAYINGS (Language Arts—Creative Thinking) The author might also have called this book *Scaredy Cats,* since the act of being scared is often associated with cats. People can easily tell when a cat is frightened—it hisses, arches its back, and puffs up its fur. Help children compile a list of other sayings that are associated with animals, for example: an elephant never forgets or slow as a snail. Children might create a story using one of these animal sayings.

IMAGINE THESE DINOSAURS (Art) Tell children they are going to create their own "helpful" dinosaurs. Using oak tag, make templates for different dinosaur body parts—heads, bodies, legs, tails. Have children choose several of these templates and trace them onto pieces of construction paper. Then have children cut out the shapes and glue them together to make their dinosaurs. Tell children to name their dinosaur and explain how it is helpful. For example, a "teacherasaurus" helps children learn. Display children's dinosaurs.

Name _____

Do You Remember?

Hello Reader!
Level 2
FRAIDY CATS
SCHOLASTIC

Cut out the pictures.
Paste them in the sentences
to tell the story.

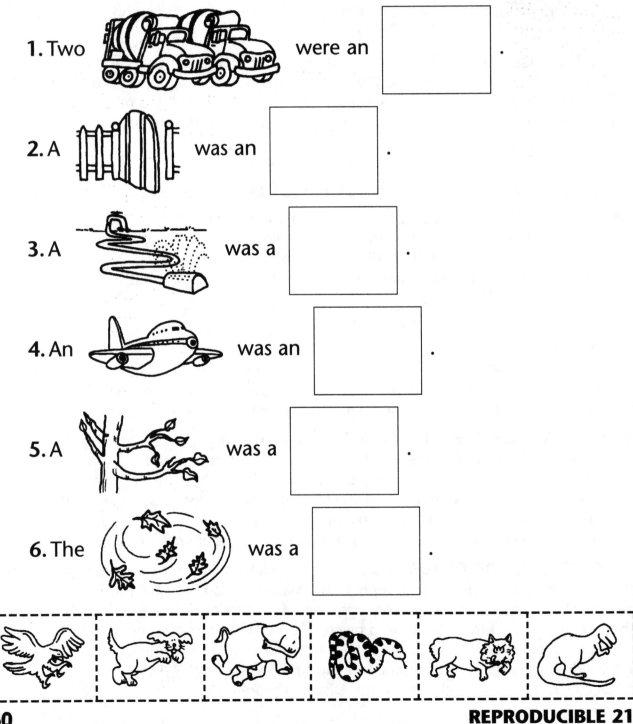

1. Two ~~[cement trucks]~~ were an _____ .

2. A ~~[gate]~~ was an _____ .

3. A ~~[sprinkler/hose]~~ was a _____ .

4. An ~~[airplane]~~ was an _____ .

5. A ~~[branch]~~ was a _____ .

6. The ~~[swirling leaves]~~ was a _____ .

THE HELLO READER! ACTIVITY BOOK   SCHOLASTIC PROFESSIONAL BOOKS

Name_____

Hello Reader!
Level 2
FRAIDY CATS
by Stephen Krensky • Illustrated by Betsy Lewin
SCHOLASTIC

Bad Night, Good Night

Some words are opposites. An opposite means what another word does not. **Hot** and **cold** are opposites. So are **good** and **bad**.

Read the words in Sorry's bed. For each word, write the opposite word in Scamper's bed. Use the words in the cap.

big
out
unfriendly
wild
fierce

SORRY

SCAMPER

small ·········· ▸ _____

gentle ·········· ▸ _____

tame ·········· ▸ _____

in ·········· ▸ _____

friendly ·········· ▸ _____

THE HELLO READER! ACTIVITY BOOK   SCHOLASTIC PROFESSIONAL BOOKS

REPRODUCIBLE 22

Great Snakes!

About This Book

Two snakes. Four snakes. Six snakes. Eight. Every single snake is great! This *Hello Science Reader!* book, written in rhyme, helps children learn many facts about different kinds of snakes. A picture glossary at the back of the book identifies each snake. The companion to this book is *Mighty Spiders!*

Themes

This book ties in well with the following themes: **Animals, Reptiles,** and **Nature.**

Meet the Author and Illustrator

Fay Robinson enjoys writing nonfiction books for young readers. As she does her research on a particular subject, she is constantly amazed that there is so much to learn and so much to write about. But Robinson always manages to make the subject accessible to young children—whether she writes in rhyme or prose. Her next *Hello Science Reader!* will be *Amazing Lizards!*

   Jean Day Zallinger has illustrated books for many years. Not only does she draw for young children, but she has illustrated college textbooks as well. Zallinger, well-known for her true-to-life style of painting, is a thorough researcher who depicts every detail in nature accurately.

Book-Related Activities

BEFORE READING Have children share their prior knowledge of snakes. Jot down on the chalkboard both the facts and misconceptions children tell you.

AFTER READING Ask students if they learned more about snakes from the book. Did anything surprise them? This might be a good time to point out that this is a nonfiction book—it gives the facts about a subject. Review the list of students' statements before they read the book. Put a star next to any statements that were found in the book. Are there any statements not found in the book? Do students think these statements are true? How can they find out? Have children add any new facts to the list that they have learned from the book.

⬛ Activities for the Reproducibles

THE FACTS, PLEASE (Science) Reproducible 23 helps children review scientific information about snakes. Tell children that they will refer back to the book as they work on this reproducible. For each sentence, they should write a book page number to prove that a statement is true or not. To extend this activity, have each child choose a fact and illustrate it. Collect children's papers, and staple them together in a book entitled, Facts About Snakes.

A GREAT SNAKE! (Art) Reproducible 24 helps children understand what it is like to be an illustrator. Be sure students have crayons, markers, scissors, string, a hole punch, and glue. Remind students that they can refer to the book as they color in their snakes. When children have cut out their snakes, help them punch a hole and loop string through it. Hang all the snakes from a clothesline strung across the classroom. Children might also use the glossary to create a key giving the name of each snake in the order it is hung.

⬛ More Cross-Curricular Activities

MY KIND OF SNAKE (Language Arts—Writing) Give children a list of categories, for example: the greatest snake, the strangest snake, the scariest snake, the best-looking snake, and the meanest snake. Have children choose one of these categories and a snake from the book that they think fits their category. Encourage children to write or dictate one or two sentences telling why they chose this snake. Allow children to share their ideas with each other by reading their sentences aloud.

FEEL THAT SKIN (Science) If possible, bring a variety of fabrics to class that resemble the scaly and smooth skins of snakes. Let children touch the fabrics and describe what they feel like. Ask children if they have ever touched the skin of a real snake. How did it feel? To extend this activity, you might bring samples of fur or feathers for children to feel. Ask them what animals these textures suggest.

A BIG BOOK OF SNAKES (Language Arts) Have children collect or draw pictures of real snakes. Or have children use the snakes on Reproducible 24 without cutting them apart. Each child should mount his or her snake on a large sheet of oak tag paper and label it. Show students how to use the glossary at the back of the book to find out the name of a snake. Choose several students to put these pages in alphabetical order and fasten them together into a Big Book. As a class, have children decide on a title. Encourage children to take the Big Book home and share it with their families.

Name _____

The Facts, Please

Read these sentences.
Put a ✔ next to each
sentence that is true.
Write the number of a page from
the book that proves your answer.

☐ **1.** Snakes have legs.   page _____

☐ **2.** Snakes hatch from eggs.   page _____

☐ **3.** Some snakes have two heads.   page _____

☐ **4.** One kind of snake can eat a crocodile.   page _____

☐ **5.** All snakes are the same size.   page _____

☐ **6.** A snake's old skin can peel right off.   page _____

REPRODUCIBLE 23

THE HELLO READER! ACTIVITY BOOK SCHOLASTIC PROFESSIONAL BOOKS

Name _____

A Great Snake!

Choose a snake from the
book that you like.
Color the snake on this
page to match.
Then cut out your snake
and hang it up.

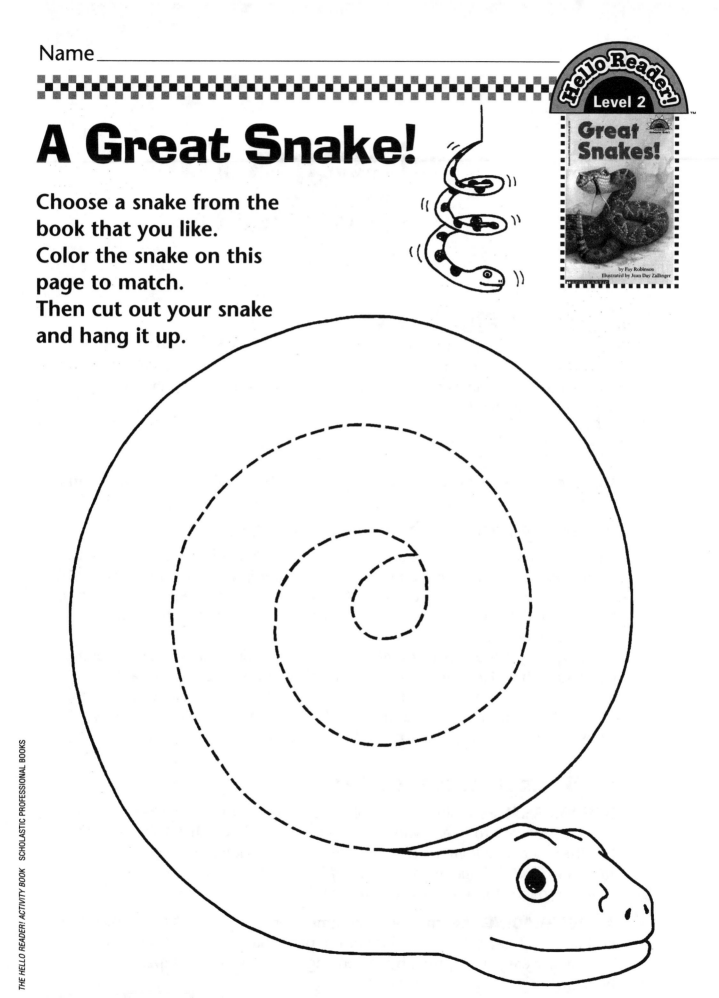

Hiccups for Elephant

About This Book

It's naptime. But Elephant is keeping all of the animals awake because he has the hiccups. His friends try to help him, but no one's remedy is successful. Finally, Mouse is able to cure Elephant's hiccups. All of the animals fall back to sleep—until Elephant lets out a great big "Ah-choo"!

Themes

This book works well with the following themes: **Animals, Health,** and **Humor.**

Meet the Author and Illustrator

James Preller understands young readers very well. He wrote this book because he knows that children find a great deal of humor in hiccups and sneezes. But his humor isn't confined to children. As soon as the Cartwheel Book editors read this manuscript, they couldn't stop laughing. They knew it would make a perfect *Hello Reader!*

Preller requested that **Hans Wilhelm** illustrate this book, so the manuscript was sent to him. However, since Wilhelm did not respond right away, the editors assumed that he didn't have time to work on the book. Surprise! In a few weeks, back came the manuscript—fully sketched out. Wilhelm really enjoyed the book, too, and agreed it would make a great *Hello Reader!*

Book-Related Activities

BEFORE READING Show the book cover to the class without reading the title. Ask children to guess who has the hiccups. How do they know? *(The word HICCUPS is coming from the elephant; animals surrounding the elephant are smiling while the elephant looks dismayed.)* Point out the speech balloon. Tell children to look for it as they read the book.

AFTER READING Ask children to comment on the book. What did they like best about it? Have children point out the parts that made the book fun to read. Then ask: Were you surprised by the ending? What were you expecting to happen?

✖ Activities for the Reproducibles

FIND THE RIGHT CURE (Reading—Understanding Details in a Story)
Reproducible 25 helps children review the details in this story. Provide scissors and glue and read the directions together with the class. When children finish working on this reproducible, have them share their ideas of how to cure Elephant's hiccups.

AND THEN... (Language Arts) Reproducible 26 provides an opportunity for children to make predictions about what might happen next. Review how the other animals acted and felt when Elephant's hiccups woke them up. Then lead a discussion of what the animals and Elephant might do next. Ask: Will Elephant be able to stop sneezing? Will the others wake up? Will they try to help Elephant? How? Will the animals ever get to finish their naps? Pass out the reproducible and have students write and illustrate the next events in the story. Invite children to share their endings with the class. Display the new endings along with the book in your reading corner.

✖ More Cross-Curricular Activities

WHAT A CHARACTER! (Reading—Fantasy vs. Reality) Discuss which animal in the story children liked best. Have children give examples from the book of why they chose this animal. Then ask children to discuss the way the illustrator portrayed this animal. Would the animal behave this way in real life? Why or why not? Ask children to point out the elements in the story that could not happen in real life.

COMIC READING (Reading) Have children bring comic strips to class. Point out the word balloons. Ask children if they know which character is speaking. How? Have children read their comic strips aloud. Encourage them to change their voices for the different characters in the strip. Then, as a class, have children write and draw their own strip. Children might enjoy using the characters in this book in their comic strip.

SOLVE IT! (Role Playing) Divide the class into groups of five. Each child in the group should be one of the animals in the book, including Elephant. Give each group a different problem to solve, such as: Elephant can't remember what he is supposed to buy at the store; Elephant's room is a mess, and he has to clean it up; Elephant is afraid of the dark. Have the other animals in the group find a solution to Elephant's problem and make up a skit. When children are ready, have them perform their skits. Have children write the name of the animal they are role playing on a piece of paper and pin it to their shirts, or have children cut out and wear paper masks of their animals.

Name_____

Find the Right Cure

Hello Reader!
Level 2
HICCUPS for Elephant
by James Preller
Illustrated by
Hans Wilhelm

Cut out the pictures.
Put a sad face next to each idea
that did not help Elephant.
Put a happy face next to the idea
that cured his hiccups.

1. Hold your breath and count to 10 . . . backward.

2. Stand on your head and eat a banana.

3. Mouse looked Elephant in the eye.
   "BOO!" he shouted.

4. Drink lots of water very, very fast.

How would you cure Elephant's hiccups?
Draw a picture or write a sentence telling how.

REPRODUCIBLE 25

And Then...

What happens next in the story?
Write your ending here.

_____

_____

_____

_____

_____

Draw a picture to go with your ending.

The 100th Day of School

▓ About This Book

The children in this class work, learn, and play. They count up to a special day. They mark their calendar until they reach the 100th day of school. On the 100th day, they do everything the 100 way—counting, measuring, multiplying, and dividing.

The 100th day of school usually occurs in the middle of the school year—somewhere between February and March.

▓ Themes

This book ties in nicely with the following themes: **School, Celebrations,** and **Holidays (Days of Special Importance).**

▓ Meet the Author and Illustrator

On one of her many visits to classrooms around the country, **Angela Shelf Medearis** found herself in a class that was celebrating the 100th day of school. She had so much fun learning about this new celebration that she called Grace Maccarone at *Hello Reader!* and told her about it. Not long after that, the idea became a new book—*The 100th Day of School.*

Artist **Joan Holub** has illustrated many school-related books throughout her career. The children in the book reflect her classroom observations and humorous touches.

▓ Book-Related Activities

BEFORE READING Ask children to tell you what they think is happening on the cover of this book. If you have been keeping track of the number of days of school, discuss how close you are to 100. Ask children to figure out how many more days are left (or have passed) until (or since) the 100th day.

AFTER READING Ask children if they would like to celebrate the 100th day of school. Have them list some activities they could do to mark that day. Keep a list of the suggestions to incorporate into your celebration.

■ Activities for the Reproducibles

WHAT IS MISSING? **(Math)** Reproducible 27 helps children understand the mathematical concept of 100. Before children start on this reproducible, you might want to review sets of 100 with them. A good way to do this is with math counters. Have children count out 100. Then have them group these items in the same combinations as in the book—50 x 2, 25 x 4, 20 x 5, and 10 x 10.

HUNT FOR 100 **(Math)** Use Reproducible 28 to help children get started on their own exploration of 100. You may want to have children work in pairs to complete the page. Challenge students to think of more ways to count, measure, or otherwise use 100.

■ More Cross-Curricular Activities

MONEY, MONEY, MONEY (Math) Since our monetary system is based on the unit of 100 ($1.00), this is a good time to teach children some money concepts. Prepare and distribute paper coins that represent pennies, nickels, dimes, and quarters. Have children count out 100 pennies, then 20 nickels, 10 dimes, and four quarters. You might want to write these as number facts in addition or subtraction problems for children to solve.

HATS ON PARADE (Art) Prepare or help children create hat shapes out of oak tag. Supply glue, scissors, markers, crayons, and stickers in the shapes of dots, squares, or stars. Have children decorate their hats, but tell them that they have to place 100 items on their hats. When children are finished, have them parade around the room wearing their "100s" hats.

TODAY IS THE DAY (Language Arts) Point out that the story is told in rhyme. Call on volunteers to identify the words that rhyme. (play/day, rule/school, day/way, one/fun, bee/tree, song/long, bin/ten, cup/up, stars/jars, store/four, twenty/plenty) Write these on the board and encourage children to add other words as well. Then have children work with partners to write a rhyming couplet about the 100th day of school. Set aside time to share students' rhymes.

Name

What Is Missing?

Look at each group below.
Circle the item that should come next.
Be sure everything adds up to 100.

Hello Reader!
Level 2

The 100th Day of School
by Angela Shelf Medearis
Illustrated by Joan Holub
SCHOLASTIC

1. ★★ ★★ ★★ ★★ ★★ ★★ ★★ ★★ ★★ ★★
   ★★ ★★ ★★ ★★ ★★ ★★ ★★ ★★ ★★ ★★
   ★★ ★★ ★★ ★★ ★★ ★★ ★★ ★★ ★★ ★★
   ★★ ★★ ★★ ★★ ★★ ★★ ★★ ★★ ★★ ★★
   ★★ ★★ ★★ ★★ ★★ ★★ ★★ ★★ ★★ ____?

   a. ★★   b. ★★★   c. ★★★★★

2. XXXXX   XXXXX   XXXXX   XXXXX
   XXXXX   XXXXX   XXXXX   XXXXX
   XXXXX   XXXXX   XXXXX   XXXXX
   XXXXX   XXXXX   XXXXX   XXXXX   ____?

   a. XXXXX   b. XXXX   c. XXX
      XXXXX   XXXX   XXX
      XXXXX   XXXX   XXX
      XXXXX   XXXX   XXX

3. ♦♦♦♦♦♦♦♦♦♦♦♦♦♦♦♦♦♦♦♦♦♦♦♦♦
   ♦♦♦♦♦♦♦♦♦♦♦♦♦♦♦♦♦♦♦♦♦♦♦♦♦
   ♦♦♦♦♦♦♦♦♦♦♦♦♦♦♦♦♦♦♦♦♦♦♦♦♦   ____?

   a. ♦ ♦ ♦ ♦   b. ♦   c. ♦ ♦ ♦
      ♦ ♦ ♦ ♦   ♦   ♦ ♦ ♦
      ♦ ♦ ♦ ♦   ♦   ♦ ♦ ♦
                        ♦   ♦ ♦ ♦

Name _____

Hello Reader!
Level 2

The 100th
Day of School

by Angela Shelf Medearis
Illustrated by Joan Holub

SCHOLASTIC

Hunt for 100

**Write your answers to the questions
on the blank lines.**

100! 100! 100! 100!

1. What number comes just before 100? _____

   Just after 100? _____

2. What is the date of the 100th day of school? _____ .

3. If you have 100 pennies, you have 1 _____ .

4. Which is more: 100 minutes or 2 hours? _____ .

5. Write 100 in words. _____

6. Show 100 with both of your hands.

   How many times did you use your hands? _____

7. Write a word for a day that is 100 degrees. _____

8. Name something you would like to have 100 of. _____

   _____

Roller Skates!

About This Book

Too many boxes of roller skates are delivered to Sam Skipper's store. So Sam decides to hold a big sale. All kinds of people buy the skates. Everyone learns that roller skates make their jobs and errands easier and more fun to do. Soon the whole town is on skates and everyone has a great time.

Themes

This book works well with the following themes: **Neighborhoods, Communities, Wheels,** and **Transportation.**

Meet the Author and Illustrator

Stephanie Calmenson started out as a teacher of young children. She then went on to work at several publishing houses but decided she wanted to write children's books full-time. Since then, she has written more than 100 books. *Roller Skates!* is a good example of how she makes reading fun for children.

True Kelley has written and illustrated many books for young children. Among them are *Look Baby! Listen Baby! Do Baby!, Let's Eat!,* and *Day Care Teddy Bear.* Kelley has also illustrated books for such authors as Joanna Cole, Franklyn Branley, Patricia Lauber, Joanne Oppenheim, and Riki Levinson. Her lighthearted illustrations add just the right touch for this book.

Book-Related Activities

BEFORE READING Ask children if they roller skate or skate in-line. Then show children the cover of this book. Has anyone ever seen a dog roller skate? What does the dog on roller skates tell them about this book? *(It's partly make-believe and probably will be funny.)*

AFTER READING What part of the story did children like best? Why? Have children cite examples. For fun, have children try to count how many people and pets are on roller skates in this book. Ask: Which of the people pictured are really likely to get around on skates? Which ones are unlikely skaters?

■ Activities for the Reproducibles

WHAT HAPPENED WHEN? (Reading—Understanding the Order of Events in a Story) Reproducible 29 helps children review the story sequence. Explain that the sentences on the reproducible are from the book. Point out that many times a writer uses certain words to help put the events of a story in order. Review order words such as, *first, second, third, soon, now, then, early,* and *later.* Can children think of other order words? You might want to keep a list in the classroom for children to refer to throughout the school year.

WHEELS GO ROUND AND ROUND (Social Studies) Because transportation is an important theme in the primary curriculum, Reproducible 30 helps children identify wheeled vehicles. Ask: Why are wheels important? *(They make things run smoothly.)* To extend this activity, have children name other vehicles that have wheels. Children can look through *Roller Skates!* and other books for ideas. Suggest that children draw or cut out pictures from magazines of these vehicles and glue them onto a chart titled *Wheels All Around Us.*

■ More Cross-Curricular Activities

BY BUS, BY CAR, BY BICYCLE (Math) Take a class survey. Have a volunteer keep track of how many children come to school by bus, car, or bicycle. How many children walk to school? skate? Are there any other ways that children get to school? Record this information on a bar graph. Ask: Which is the most popular way of coming to school? How do you know?

WHO ELSE USES ROLLER SKATES? (Writing) Have children think of and add another scene to this book. Divide the class into small groups. Some children could collaborate on the text while others work together on the illustration. Have the groups share their scenes. Then post them on a classroom bulletin board.

NEIGHBORHOOD SCENES (Social Studies) Throughout this book are some great neighborhood scenes. The action takes place in the downtown shopping area, on the sidewalks in front of people's homes, in the park, and along the town's streets. Have children discuss and then work together to create a street map of their neighborhood. Ask: Where are the stores? the school? the park? people's homes? What other buildings or areas are there? What vehicles are used to help people get around? Children might add these to their map. Display the map in a prominent place in the classroom.

Name_____

What Happened When?

Read the groups of sentences. Put them in the correct order. Write the numbers 1, 2, 3, and 4 on the blank lines. Then draw a picture for each group.

a.

_____ People came from far and wide. There were even people who never had tried to get around on roller skates.

b.

_____ Early one morning in a small sleepy town, six trucks rumbled up and boxes came down.

c.

_____ Soon an idea popped into Sam's head. He made up a sign and here's what it said: BIG SALE TODAY ON ROLLER SKATES!

d.

_____ Now in this lively town, all the people agree that life is as easy as it can be . . . when everyone rides on roller skates!

Name _____

Wheels Go Round and Round

Which ones need wheels?
Draw wheels on the ones that use them.
Then color the pictures.

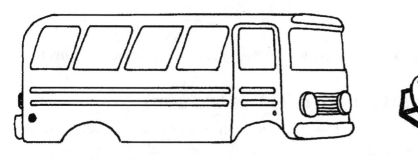
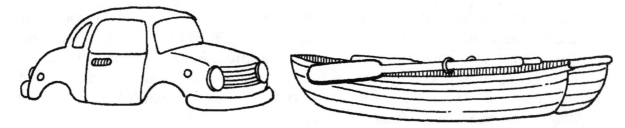
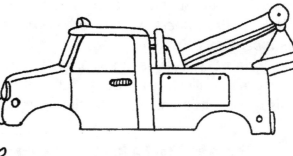

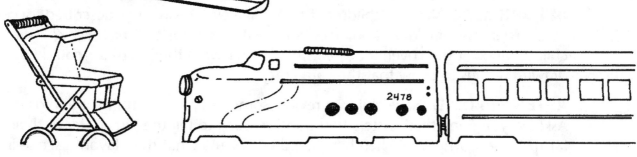

Hello Reader!
Level 2

Two Crazy Pigs

by Karen Berman Nagel
Illustrated by Brian Schatell

Two Crazy Pigs

About This Book

Two crazy pigs lived on the Fensters' farm. But they were so mischievous that the Fensters told them to leave. The pigs found a new home on the Henhawks' farm where they could be as crazy as they wanted. But the animals on the Fensters' farm missed them so much. When the Fensters moved to the city, all of the animals came to live with the two pigs on the Henhawks' farm. And, of course, everything was as zany as ever!

Themes

You can use this book with the following themes: **Farm Animals** and **Humor.**

Meet the Author and Illustrator

At one time, **Karen Berman Nagel** worked on staff at Avon Books. When she left her staff position, she became a freelance writer for Scholastic Inc., as well as other publishers. Among the books she has written are *On the Lunch Line Hello Math Reader!, Norfin Trolls Camp Out,* and *Three Young Maniacs and the Red Rubber Boots. Two Crazy Pigs* is her favorite story.

Brian Schatell began as an intern in an advertising agency but went on to become an illustrator. Today, Schatell continues to illustrate children's books and also works as a children's textile designer.

Book-Related Activities

BEFORE READING Ask children if they have ever heard pigs described as crazy. Then ask if children think this book will be serious or funny. Why? Have children look at the cover and brainstorm other ways the illustrator could have drawn the pigs to show that they are crazy.

AFTER READING Have children review some of the crazy things the pigs did. Ask: Do you think the Fensters had good reasons to tell the pigs to leave their farm? Why or why not? Then have children discuss what their favorite scene in the book was and explain why.

⚡ Activities for the Reproducibles

JUST DO IT! (**Language Arts**) Reproducible 31 gives children practice in recognizing and using verbs. Call on a volunteer to read the sentences aloud. You might want to do the first sentence as an example. When children are finished working on this reproducible, choose several of them to act out the sentences. Children should be able to evaluate their own papers.

MORE CRAZY PIGS (**Language Arts—Speaking and Listening**) Students can make the crazy pig mask on Reproducible 32 to wear when reporting to the class on the book. Have children color and cut out their masks. Provide string or yarn to help secure the masks. Suggest that children work with a partner so there are two crazy pigs to review the book for the class. Remind students to support their statements with evidence from the book.

⚡ More Cross-Curricular Activities

WHAT WOULD HAPPEN IF? (**Language Arts—Writing**) Have children think about what would happen at the end of the book if the two crazy pigs did visit the Fensters in the city. Encourage children to write or dictate a paragraph or draw a picture showing their thoughts. Have children share their ideas.

ANIMAL FARM (**Reading—Comparing and Contrasting**) Have children compare this book to another book they have read about animals that live on a farm, for example, *The Cows Are in the Corn* or *"Buzz," Said the Bee*. Help children make a Venn diagram. In the overlapping area of the circles, have children list all of the similarities found in the two books, such as the same animals that live on the farms. If the animals are not the same, then place the names of these animals in the corresponding circles (for instance, the left side for *The Cows Are in the Corn* and the right side for *Two Crazy Pigs*). Post this diagram in the reading corner. Encourage children to compare and contrast other books about farm animals as they read them.

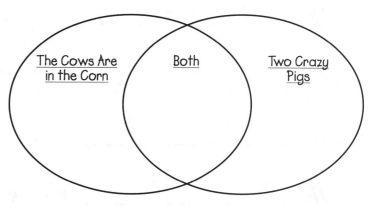

HOME SWEET HOME (**Art**) Mr. Henhawk created a new pigpen for the two crazy pigs. Have children choose one or more animals and make a home for it (them). Provide children with clay, blocks, building toys, construction paper, sticks, dried leaves, glue, scissors, and any other items that could be used to make a good home.

Name _____

Just Do It!

Read each sentence.
Add an action word from the
barn to tell what the pigs did.

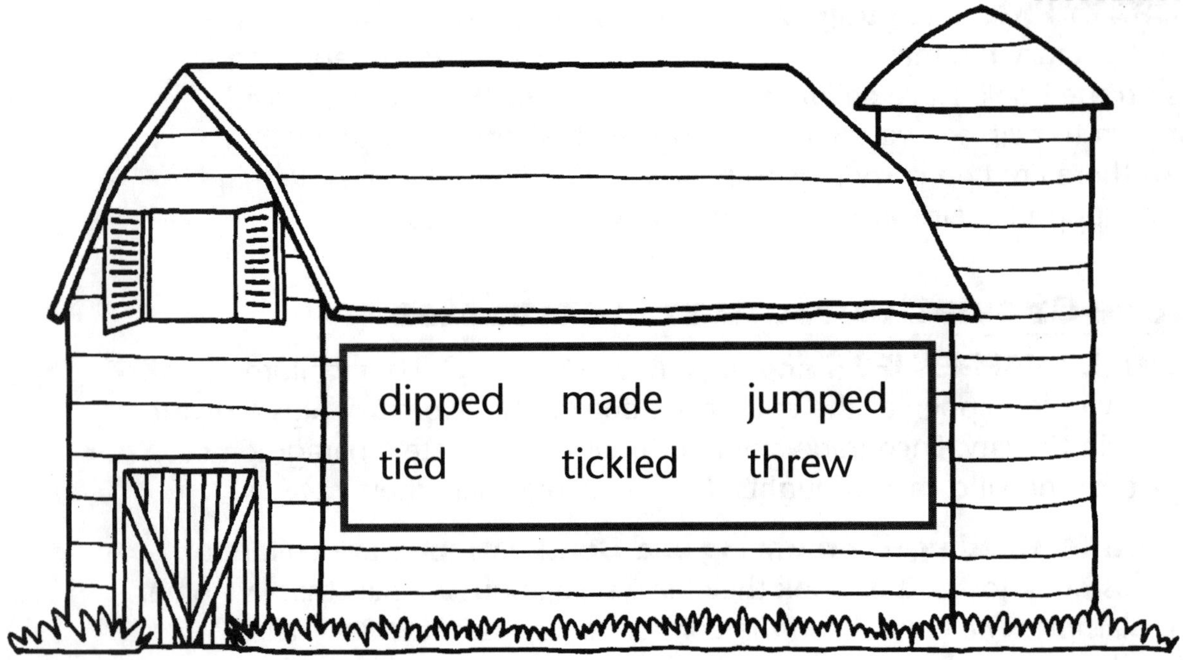

| dipped | made | jumped |
| tied | tickled | threw |

1. We _____ the hens.

2. We _____ the cows' tails together.

3. We _____ mud at each other.

4. We _____ the sheep's tail in ink.

5. We _____ mud pies in the stove.

6. We _____ on the bed for two hours.

REPRODUCIBLE 31

Name _____

More Crazy Pigs

Color the crazy pig mask.
Then cut it out.
Add string and put it on.

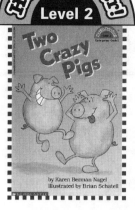

Wake Me in Spring

About This Book

Mouse loves winter. He can't wait to share it with his best friend, Bear. But Bear has something to do during the winter; he has to sleep. Mouse will miss Bear and Bear will miss Mouse. But Bear gives Mouse a great big bear hug—one that is large enough to last all winter. Mouse tucks Bear into bed and promises to wake him in spring when flowers bloom and best friends sing.

Themes

This book works well with the following themes: **Bears, Animals, Winter, Seasons,** and **Friendship.**

Meet the Author and Illustrator

James Preller and **Jeffrey Scherer** both live in Albany, New York, with their families. James Preller is a freelance author and editor who has written such books as *Hiccups for Elephant* and *Meet the Authors and Illustrators, Volumes One and Two.* Jeffrey Scherer is a freelance artist who works on *The Albany Times* newspaper. In addition to illustrating *Wake Me in Spring,* Jeffrey Scherer has written and illustrated *One Snowy Day,* a Level 1 *Hello Reader!*

Book-Related Activities

BEFORE READING Show children the cover of the book. Read the title. Ask children what they think the title means. *(One of the animals may be going to sleep for the winter.)* Have children guess which animal might need to be awakened in the spring? Why?

AFTER READING Have children describe how this book made them feel. Did they understand Bear's point of view? Mouse's point of view? Have children share their favorite scene in the book.

▚ Activities for the Reproducibles

TALKING TOGETHER (Creative Dramatics) Use the patterns on Reproducible 33 to make stick puppets of Bear and Mouse. Have children color and cut out the puppets, then glue them to wooden craft sticks. Children can work with partners to reenact the story. Encourage them to read the dialogue from the book. Children might also enjoy cutting out or drawing pictures of their favorite winter activities and gluing them onto a long sheet of butcher paper. Title this mural *During the Winter, We Love to ___.*

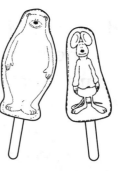

HUG, HUG ME TRUE (Letter Writing) Reproducible 34 gives children practice in writing friendly letters. Point out the parts of a friendly letter—date, greeting, body, closing, signature. Tell children that they should write a rough draft of their letter, edit it, and then rewrite it on the reproducible. Students can make or address standard envelopes and mail their letters.

▚ More Cross-Curricular Activities

WAKE UP, IT'S SPRING! (Language Arts—Writing) Have children think about the day that Mouse wakes up Bear. What do children think that Bear and Mouse will do that day? How do they think Bear and Mouse will feel? Encourage children to dictate, or write, and illustrate a story that describes their thoughts. Have children share their stories. Ask children if anyone used the clues on the last page of the book and had Bear and Mouse go fishing together.

IT'S WINTER, THEN IT'S SPRING (Comparing and Contrasting) Since this book touches on two seasons, have children think about the characteristics of each. Help children make a comparison chart by dividing chart paper into two columns, *Winter* and *Spring.* Ask: How do these seasons differ? Are there any similarities? When students finish, take a class vote to find out which of these seasons is the class favorite.

WHO SLEEPS DURING THE WINTER? (Science) Explain to children that when Bear goes to sleep during the winter, it is called *hibernation.* Help children understand that bears are not the only animals that sleep through the winter. Woodchucks, lizards, frogs, toads, turtles, and some snakes also hibernate. Help children look through books about animals to find out where these animals sleep. If possible, have children draw or photocopy pictures of these animals and their homes. Children can label these pictures and staple them together into a book titled *Good Night for the Winter.*

Talking Together

Color Bear and Mouse.
Then cut them out and
glue them to craft sticks.

Name _____

Hello Reader!
Level 2

Hug, Hug Me True

Bear gave Mouse a hug to last all winter.
Send a hug letter to someone you care about—
a friend, a classmate, or a family member.

Wake Me in Spring

by Janice Preller
Illustrated by Jeffrey Scherer

SCHOLASTIC

_____ , 19 _____

Dear _____ ,

Here's a big hug for you. I hope it will

_____

_____

_____

_____

_____

_____

All my hugs,

_____

Endangered Animals

■ About This Book

This book teaches an important lesson to young children: many animals in the world today are becoming endangered. As humans take up more space, there is less room for animals to live safely and raise their young. The book points out that endangered animals need help, including laws to protect them from hunters and developers. Children learn that when people save a homeland for animals, they save something wonderful for themselves—the beautiful natural world.

■ Themes

This book ties in nicely with the following themes: **Endangered Animals, Environment, Earth,** and **Animals.**

■ Meet the Author and Illustrator

Faith McNulty has won many awards for her books on animals and nature. She enjoys explaining the natural world to young readers. McNulty is the author of such books as *Orphan—The Story of a Baby Woodchuck, A Snake in the House,* and the *Hello Reader! Dancing With Manatees.*

   Carol Schwartz's realistic paintings have great appeal for young readers. Among the many books she has illustrated are four books in Cartwheel's *Hide and Seek Science* series—*Where's That Fish?, Where's That Reptile?, Where's That Insect?,* and *Where's That Cat?*

■ Book-Related Activities

BEFORE READING Have children define the word *endangered*. Ask: How does it make you feel when you hear that some animals are endangered? Tell children that this book not only tells about endangered animals but also gives suggestions about how people can protect them.

AFTER READING Review what children learned. What are some extinct animals? What are some endangered animals? Discuss the reasons why animals become endangered or extinct and what people can do to prevent this.

▪ Activities for the Reproducibles

LEARNING MORE (Social Studies) Reproducible 35 asks children to research and answer questions about an endangered animal. Be sure to have nonfiction books, encyclopedias, children's nature magazines, and other resources available. Before children start working, review the questions on the reproducible with them. If children have any difficulty, divide them into small groups to work together to find the answers. To help children get started, suggest that they choose one of the following animals to research: whooping crane, California condor, Asian rhinoceros, or manatee. Save children's answers to use with the activity Where in the World?, in the More Cross-Curricular Activities section.

WHAT SHOULD WE DO? (Critical Thinking) Reproducible 36 is a role-playing activity in which children use their critical-thinking skills. Divide the class into groups of six. Have children color and cut out the badges. Each child chooses one badge. Help children pin on the badge, or punch a hole and put the badge on a string for children to wear around their necks. Give children this problem: There is a vacant lot with many trees on it. The trees are home to different birds. A family wants to cut down the trees to build a house. The builder and town official support them. Have children think about what their characters would say. Then have them role-play their ideas. When everyone is finished, take a vote on whether the house should be built.

▪ More Cross-Curricular Activities

WHERE IN THE WORLD? (Social Studies) Direct children's attention to the last page of the book. Explain that parts of three continents are shown—North America, South America, and Africa. Have children identify the endangered animals on this page. Then using a map of the world posted in your classroom, write the names of these endangered animals and any others children know on small pieces of paper. (Children can refer to their answers to Reproducible 35.) Pin the names of the animals onto the correct continents. Students might draw pictures of these animals on small sticky notes and add the pictures to the map.

ANIMALS SPEAK OUT (Creative Dramatics) Divide children into small groups. Give each group the name of a different endangered animal. Have children prepare a skit about what these animals might say to each other about the world they live in. You might also have children choose a narrator from each group to describe what the world would be like if the animal became extinct. Give each group a chance to perform its skit.

Name _____

Learning More

Choose an endangered animal.
Answer these questions.

Endangered
Animals

My endangered animal is _____.

This animal lives _____

_____.

It is endangered because _____

_____

_____.

This is what my animal looks like. Draw or cut out a picture.

REPRODUCIBLE 35

Name_____

What Should We Do?

Color in these badges.
Then cut them out.

FOR

Family

FOR

Builder

FOR

Town Official

AGAINST

Child

AGAINST

Scientist

AGAINST

Bird Watcher

Germs! Germs! Germs!

About This Book

We're on the ground. We're in the air. We're GERMS and we live everywhere! So begins this rollicking *Hello Science Reader!* told from the germs' point of view. Without realizing it, though, readers learn how to take care of themselves and how to prevent illnesses by following some simple health tips.

Themes

This book fits in with the following themes: **Health** and **All About Me.**

Meet the Author and Illustrator

Bobbi Katz is a renowned children's poet with a great sense of humor. She can teach any subject to children because she knows how to speak to them. Bobbi Katz has written many volumes of poetry, including *Ghosts and Goose Bumps, Poems to Chill Your Bones,* and *Upside Down and Inside Out: Poems for All Your Pockets.* Her latest book for Cartwheel Books is called *Truck Talk—Rhymes on Wheels.*

   Steve Björkman said he had a wonderful time illustrating *Germs! Germs! Germs!* because he could be as creative as he wanted. Björkman has illustrated many books for Scholastic Press, including *I Hate English* (an ALA Notable Book), *In 1942, In 1776, This Is the Way We Go to School,* and *This Is the Way We Eat Our Lunch.* He also illustrated another *Hello Science Reader!* titled *A Book About Your Skeleton.*

Book-Related Activities

BEFORE READING Show children the cover. Explain that germs are microscopic, which means that they can't be seen except under a microscope. Point out that for this book the illustrator has made the germs bigger than they really are. Ask children if they think germs have eyes, noses, and mouths? Why do they think the illustrator drew them this way? Tell children to look for the ways people can protect themselves from germs as they read this book.

AFTER READING Encourage children to share their responses to this book. *(Elicit responses such as, funny, silly, germs do a lot of things, germs cause many illnesses, I can protect myself from germs.)* Then have children name some things they learned about germs from the book.

Activities for the Reproducibles

STAY WELL (Understanding Details) Reproducible 37 reinforces what children have learned from reading this book. Children will be making a mini-book of tips on how to stay well. Have children draw and color a picture that illustrates each sentence. Then have children cut out each page and staple the pages together. Children can take their mini-books home and share them with their families.

Stay Well: Tips for Keeping Germs Away

FRIENDS OR FOES? (Reading Comprehension) By working on Reproducible 38, children use the information they have learned from the book. You might follow up by asking them to pretend they are germs. How do they feel when as germs they are kept out? Children can draw a picture of themselves as germs on the back of the reproducible.

More Cross-Curricular Activities

MICROSCOPIC GERMS (Science) If possible, bring a microscope with several slides to class. Have children look at the slides. Can they tell what is on the slide? Point out the different magnifications that are on the microscope. Ask children which one(s) help them to see more clearly. If you can, round up slides with germs on them. Do the germs under the microscope look like the germs in the book? Why or why not?

CAN YOU FIND THE RHYME? (Language Arts) This book is written in rhyme. Have children look through the book and find the rhyming words. If you have rhyming word charts in your classroom, have children help you add the words they find to the correct charts. Can children add words to each group of words? Encourage children to refer to these charts whenever they have a writing assignment in which they are asked to write in rhyme.

WHAT DO YOU DO WHEN YOU GET SICK? (Health) This book gives good tips on how to prevent illnesses. Hold a class discussion and review these preventive measures. Then have children talk about what they should do when they're not feeling well. *(Tell a grown-up. Visit the doctor. Follow the doctor's orders. Take all medications that are prescribed. Rest. Eat well.)*

Name _____

Stay Well

Read the sentences. Draw a picture for each sentence. Cut out the pages and put them together to make a book.

**Stay Well:
Tips for
Keeping
Germs Away**

Wash your hands.

Get plenty of fresh air
and sunshine.

Keep food fresh.

Cover your cough
and sneeze, please.

Eat healthful foods.

THE HELLO READER! ACTIVITY BOOK   SCHOLASTIC PROFESSIONAL BOOKS

Name _____

Friends or Foes?

Germs like these people.
Tell what each person should
do to keep germs away.

1. Sneezer _____

_____

2. Finger Licker _____

_____

3. Meal Skipper _____

_____

4. Nose Picker _____

_____

5. Hurry Ups _____

_____

A Girl Named Helen Keller

About This Book

This biography of Helen Keller gives details about her life when she was a young girl. At the age of two, Helen Keller became blind and deaf from a serious childhood illness. Her parents could not communicate with her, so they could not teach her. Eventually, they found Anne Sullivan, who came from the Perkins Institution for the Blind. Although it took Anne Sullivan a long time to reach Helen Keller, she was finally able to help her "crack the code" for recognizing words by devising a method of manual spelling. From her earliest days, Helen Keller was remarkable, as was the rest of her life.

Another book that children might enjoy reading in this *Hello Reader!* mini-series of biographies is *A Boy Named Boomer* by NFL Quarterback Boomer Esiason.

Themes

This book works well with the following themes: **Famous People or Famous Women, Facing Challenges, Problem Solving, Friendship,** and **Families.**

Meet the Author and Illustrator

Margo Lundell once worked as a children's book editor, but now she writes children's books full-time. Her many books include *The Furry Bedtime Book* for Cartwheel Books and the new *Hello Reader!* mini-series—*Lad a Dog: Lad to the Rescue, Lad a Dog: Best Dog in the World, Lad a Dog: Lad Is Lost,* and *Lad a Dog: Lad and the Bad Puppy.*

Irene Trivas is well-known for the beautiful portraits she paints. She thoroughly researches all of her subjects. She is the illustrator of *My First Book of Biographies* for Cartwheel Books.

Book-Related Activities

BEFORE READING Ask if anyone knows who Helen Keller was. Have children look at the cover of the book. Choose a volunteer to read the title. Based on the title, have another child point to Helen Keller. How did this child know who to point to? *(Elicit the response that the title has the word* girl *in it.)* Tell children that the woman on the cover is Helen Keller's teacher, Anne Sullivan. Ask children to read to find out why these women were so remarkable.

AFTER READING What did children think of Helen Keller? How did they feel when she understood what "w-a-t-e-r" meant? Ask children to name some words that they think describe Helen Keller. Keep a list of these words. Ask children if they have ever experienced the same feelings as Helen Keller did. Ask: How did you feel when you were learning to read? How did you feel when you realized you could read? Invite children to provide other example.

Activities for the Reproducibles

A HELEN KELLER TIMELINE (Reading—Sequence) Reproducible 39 gives students a chance to review the sequence of events in Helen Keller's life. Encourage students to look back in the book if they need to. When students finish, invite them to make a large timeline of Helen Keller's life to display in the classroom. Suggest that students add more events to the class timeline.

SPECIAL SIGNS (Decoding) Reproducible 40 helps children decode *The One-Hand Manual Alphabet* at the back of the book. Make sure there are enough copies of the alphabet for children to use as they work on this reproducible.

More Cross-Curricular Activities

FURTHER READING (Reading) Children may want to learn more about Helen Keller. If so, encourage them to go to the school or town library and choose another book about Helen Keller. Or you might want to set aside time each day to read an appropriate chapter book about Helen Keller aloud to the class.

CRACK THE CODE (Problem Solving) Children might enjoy solving other codes. Make up sentences or stories using rebus pictures and hand them out to the class. Have children work alone or in small groups to "read" these sentences. For example:

① day the 🧍 went ⬇ the ⌇.

One day the girl went down the slide.

SAY IT WITH YOUR HANDS (Social Studies) Give children a chance to use *The One-Hand Manual Alphabet* at the back of the book. Tell each child to think of a word and spell it using this alphabet. When children have practiced their words and feel proficient using the alphabet, have each child "speak" the word. The class can try to figure out what the word is. If possible, show children an example of a book printed in Braille so that students can begin to understand how Helen Keller was able to read.

Name_____

A Helen Keller Timeline

Hello Reader!
Level 3
A Girl Named Helen Keller
by Margo Lundell
Illustrated by Irene Trivas
SCHOLASTIC

Cut out the sentences about Helen Keller's life.
Paste them in order on the timeline.

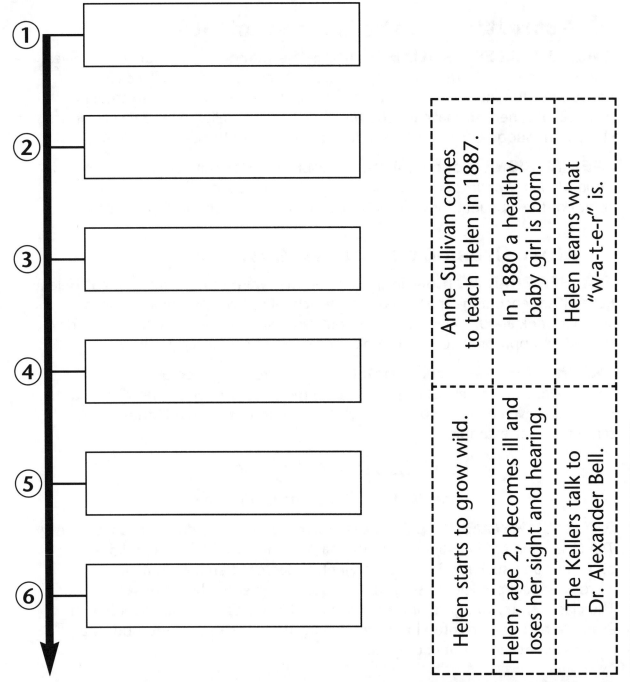

1
2
3
4
5
6

Anne Sullivan comes to teach Helen in 1887.

In 1880 a healthy baby girl is born.

Helen learns what "w-a-t-e-r" is.

Helen starts to grow wild.

Helen, age 2, becomes ill and loses her sight and hearing.

The Kellers talk to Dr. Alexander Bell.

THE HELLO READER! ACTIVITY BOOK SCHOLASTIC PROFESSIONAL BOOKS

REPRODUCIBLE 39

Special Signs

Use **The One-Hand Manual Alphabet**
at the back of the book.
Write each letter on the blank line.

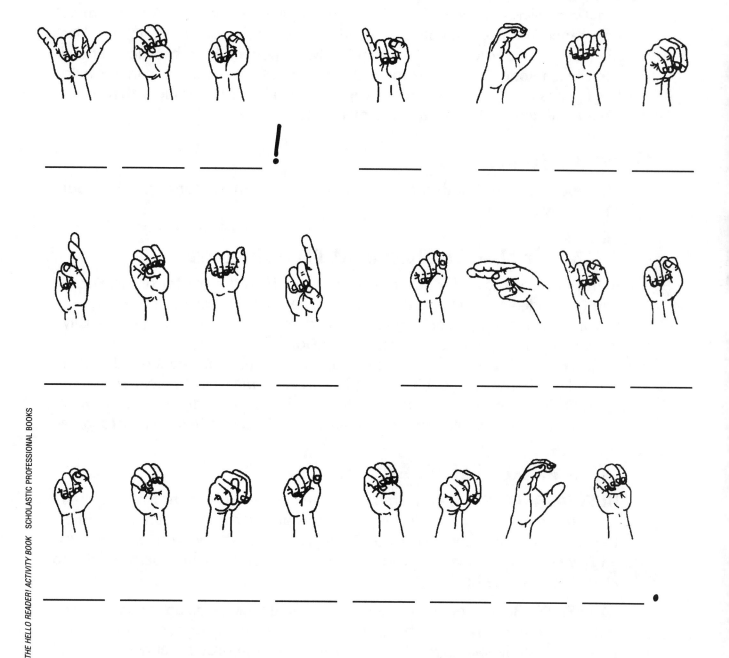

___ ___ ___ ___ ! ___ ___ ___ ___

___ ___ ___ ___   ___ ___ ___ ___

___ ___ ___ ___ ___ ___ ___ ___ .

Hello Reader!

Level 3

Monster
Manners

by Joanna Cole
Illustrated by Jared Lee

Monster Manners

About This Book

What are monster parents to do when their only monster child does not mind her manners? Rosie's parents try everything, but Rosie just can't catch on. Her manners aren't monstrous at all; they're always perfect! Even her friend Prunella can't teach Rosie monster manners. But one day, Rosie's perfect manners help her parents out of a bad situation. Then they realize just how lucky they are to have a daughter with such strange manners!

Themes

This book works well with the following themes: **Humor, Manners, All About Me**, and **Monsters**.

Meet the Author and Illustrator

Joanna Cole is known for her sense of humor. She is the creator of Ms. Frizzle and the students in *The Magic School Bus* series of books. She is a thorough researcher who enjoys teaching young children new things. But she especially loves it when children have a good time reading her books.

Jared Lee also likes to know that young children are having a good time. He is the illustrator of such books as *The Teacher From the Black Lagoon, The Principal From the Black Lagoon,* and *The Gym Teacher From the Black Lagoon,* as well as a new four-book series for Cartwheel Books called *Happily Ever Laughter.*

Book-Related Activities

BEFORE READING Ask children if anyone has ever told them that they had "monster manners"? What do they think this phrase means? Then ask children to predict what this book will be about by looking at the artwork on the cover and by reading the title. Jot down students' ideas on the chalkboard to refer to after they read the book.

AFTER READING Review students' ideas. Were their predictions correct? What did children think about this book? Did children learn what good manners are? How do other people respond to good manners? to monster manners?

▚ Activities for the Reproducibles

PRUNELLA AND ROSIE (Reading—Understanding Characters) Although Rosie and Prunella are both monsters, they are quite different. Reproducible 41 helps children to better understand these characters by comparing them. Students will need scissors and paste as they work on this reproducible. To extend this activity, have children tell you how Rosie and Prunella would behave at the movies, in a store, or in school.

SAY IT! (Understanding Dialogue) Reproducible 42 gives children practice in identifying and writing dialogue. Before students begin working on this reproducible, ask them how they can tell when a character in a book is speaking. *(Children should be able to point out verbs, such as* said, asked, answered, replied, *and* cried *as well as the quotation marks around the words that are being spoken.)* Go over the directions with the class and model how to use quotation marks. When children finish working on this reproducible, have them write a dialogue between two people. Remind them to use quotation marks and verbs in their sentences.

▚ More Cross-Curricular Activities

MIND YOUR MANNERS (Social Studies) Ask children why they think it is important to have good manners. Have children help you make a list of good manners to post on a bulletin board. Children might enjoy illustrating this list. Then, after a few weeks, have the class vote on who has the best classroom manners, the best table manners, the best manners in general.

A MONSTROUSLY FUN TIME (Creative Dramatics) This book is a lot of fun to act out. Choose students to play the parts of the different characters. These children might enjoy making paper-bag puppets of their characters to use as they perform. Since the book is long, you might want to choose two students for each part. Students could change roles midway through the book.

MY FAVORITE MONSTER (Writing) Have children create their own monsters. Encourage children to be as creative as possible. Give these guidelines: What does your monster look like? Is your monster friendly, scary, normal, strange, happy, sad, mean, or sweet? What other words can you use to describe your monster? What does your monster do? Does your monster have a family? Does your monster have friends? Enemies? Have children draw their monster and write a short story about it. Remind children to give their monster a name and to use dialogue in their stories. When children are ready, have them share their stories. Then put all of the stories together in a classroom book titled *A Monstrous Book About Monsters*.

Name_____

Prunella and Rosie

Cut out the faces below.
Paste Prunella or Rosie next to
the sentences that tell about them.

1. She threw her food all around the restaurant.

5. She brushed her teeth after her first bite of a rock.

2. She said, "How do you do?" and sat quietly on the sofa.

6. She kicked the dog high in the sky.

3. She jumped up and down on her uncle's favorite chair.

7. She knocked so hard that the door fell down.

4. She spoke in a nice voice.

8. She helped an old man cross the street.

90

REPRODUCIBLE 41

THE HELLO READER! ACTIVITY BOOK   SCHOLASTIC PROFESSIONAL BOOKS

Name_____

Monster Manners

by Joanna Cole
Illustrated by Jared Lee

Say It!

Read the speech balloons.
Then write each sentence
on the correct line below.
Use quotation marks.
An example is done for you.

Mind your
manners, dear.

May I see the
menu, please?

I'm afraid Rosie
will never learn.

I'll be right there.

PLUMBER

I did my best, Rosie.

1. Mother said, _"Mind your manners, dear."_

2. Prunella said, _____

3. Father said, _____

4. The plumber said, _____

5. Rosie said, _____

The Popcorn Shop

About This Book

Popcorn Nell's popcorn is so popular that she can't make enough to sell. The solution is a large machine that does the popping. But, one day, something goes wrong, and the machine makes way too much popcorn. Everything in Nell's town comes to a halt because there is so much popcorn everywhere. Finally the machine blows its top. That's when Popcorn Nell decides to become Pizza Nell. "With pizza, nothing can go wrong!" Nell exclaims. Or can it?

Themes

This book fits in well with the following themes: **Humor**, **Food**, **Communities**, and **Neighborhoods**.

Meet the Author and Illustrator

Alice Low is a children's book author as well as a playwright. Among the two dozen books she has written are *Mommy's Briefcase* (a novelty book for young children) and *Witches' Holiday*.

For many years **Patti Hammel** was a full-time illustrator at Hallmark Cards. *The Popcorn Shop* was one of the first books she worked on when she decided to become a freelance illustrator. She also illustrated *All About the Seasons Activity Book* for Scholastic Inc.

Book-Related Activities

BEFORE READING Take a vote—how many children like popcorn? Do they like it plain? with butter? with salt? warm or cold? Graph students' responses.

AFTER READING Now take another vote—how many children like pizza? Do they like it plain? with a topping? If so, what are the more popular toppings? Make another graph of students' responses. Then have students compare the popcorn graph to the pizza graph. Ask questions such as: Which is the more popular food? How many children like it? How many more (or fewer) children like pizza with pepperoni than pizza with peppers? How many children like buttered popcorn?

Activities for the Reproducibles

UP AND DOWN WORDS (Language Arts—Vocabulary) Reproducible 43 encourages children to use the vocabulary words from the story. Review with students how to fill in a crossword puzzle. Tell children that all of the words are from the book. If children can't figure out the words, encourage them to look back at the book to find these words.

POP, POP, POPPING ALL AROUND (Creative Writing) Reproducible 44 asks children to use their creative-thinking and writing skills. As children look at this reproducible, have them think of things to say that are based on the humor in the book. To extend this activity, have children use the characters and what they say as the basis for writing or dictating a story. Have students read their stories aloud.

More Cross-Curricular Activities

THE PIZZA SHOP (Language Arts—Writing) Using *The Popcorn Shop* as a model, have children collaborate and write a story about Pizza Nell's Pizza Shop. What might happen to the pizza? Where in the neighborhood might it travel? As students tell you their ideas, write them on the chalkboard. Then ask volunteers to write and/or illustrate different pages for the book. Children can work in pairs for each page. If writing in rhyme is too difficult, encourage children to write in prose. When children are satisfied with their work, have them put all the pages together in a book and design a cover. Place the book in the classroom library.

A POPCORN PARTY (Cooking) Have children plan a popcorn party. If possible, bring a popcorn maker to class so children can watch the popcorn pop. You might try the following recipe to make popcorn balls.

- **Materials and Ingredients:** popcorn, popcorn popper, bowl, 2 cups molasses, saucepan, stirring spoon, butter, wax paper
- **Directions:** Prepop the corn. Cook the molasses over medium heat, stirring often, until a test drop hardens in cold water (about 10 to 15 minutes). Pour the molasses over the popcorn and stir. When the molasses is cool enough, let children coat their hands with butter and form the popcorn into balls. Set the balls on wax paper to cool. Eat!

DECORATE WITH POPCORN (Art) Have children string popcorn to make decorations. Have plenty of thread, needles, and scissors on hand. You might also have cranberries and other fruits available to string with the popcorn. Have volunteers decorate the classroom.

Name _____

Up and Down Words

Read the sentences from the book.
Write the missing word in the puzzle boxes.

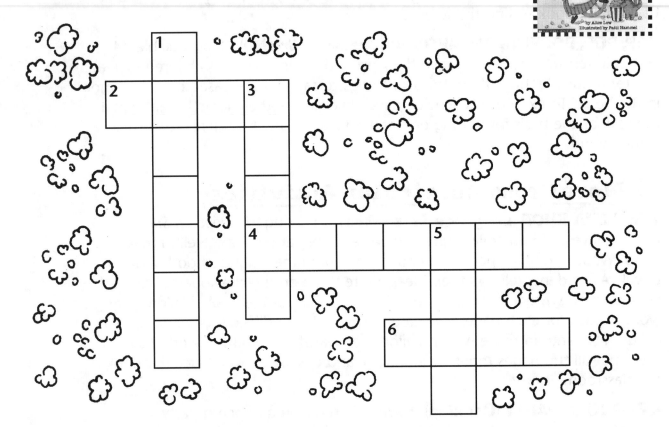

Across

2. Now there was plenty in the _____ until that machine broke down.

4. And everybody cried, "Hooray! Let's have a popcorn _____!"

6. It popped the popcorn all day long, and as it popped, Nell sang this _____.

Down

1. Popcorn Nell had a _____ shop.

3. And sure enough that man was right. The popcorn popped both day and _____.

5. The popcorn popped onto the floor, and then it popped right out the _____.

94

REPRODUCIBLE 43

THE HELLO READER! ACTIVITY BOOK SCHOLASTIC PROFESSIONAL BOOKS

Pop, Pop, Popping All Around

Look at this picture.
Write what each person would say.

Hello Reader!
Level 3

THE POPCORN SHOP
FRESH POPCORN HOT
by Alice Low
Illustrated by Patti Hammel

School Friends: The Best Teacher in the World

■ About This Book

When Ms. Darcy chooses Bunny Rabissi to take a note to Mrs. Walker, Bunny is so excited that she forgets to ask where Mrs. Walker's classroom is. Rather than go back and look foolish in front of Ms. Darcy and her classmates, Bunny decides to look for Mrs. Walker's room by herself. But she never finds it and so she never delivers the note. Worse than that, Bunny lies and tells Ms. Darcy that she did give the note to Mrs. Walker. Bunny feels terrible about what she did. By the end of the book, Bunny learns an important lesson—never be afraid to ask a question when you don't know something.

Children might enjoy reading another book by the same authors in this *Hello Reader!* series, *School Friends: Martin and the Teacher's Pets*.

■ Themes

This book fits in well with the following themes: **School, All About Me,** and **Problem Solving**.

■ Meet the Authors and Illustrator

Bernice Chardiet runs an editorial and book packaging company. She is responsible for bringing many successful book projects to Cartwheel Books, including the *Hide-and-Seek Science* series. She enjoyed collaborating with **Grace Maccarone** on the *School Friends* series, since they could share stories from their own childhoods with each other as well as with their readers.

G. Brian Karas is the illustrator of more than 30 books for children. Among them are *I Know an Old Lady; Like Butter on Pancakes, Eeek! Stories to Make You Shriek, Squeaky Shoes,* and *Please Raise Your Hand: Poems about School.* Karas's work has also appeared in *The New York Times* and *Parents* magazine. He is known for his offbeat sense of humor and quirky illustrations.

◼ Book-Related Activities

BEFORE READING Based on the cover, ask children where they think this book takes place. What clues did they use? Ask: How would you describe the best teacher in the world? What qualities would this teacher have?

AFTER READING Discuss how Bunny's feelings of inadequacy caused her to do something she knew was wrong. Ask: Why was Bunny wrong? Why was she brave? Why was Ms. Darcy very, very smart? Why did Bunny think she was the best teacher in the world? Then invite children to share their thoughts about what they would have done in Bunny Rabissi's situation. Have children give reasons for their answers. Ask children if anything like this has ever happened to them. How was it the same? Different?

◼ Activities for the Reproducibles

WHERE IS MRS. WALKER? (Following Directions) Reproducible 45 reinforces children's ability to follow directions. To extend this activity, have children choose a spot in the classroom and write directions for a classmate to follow to reach that spot. Children should realize that their directions have to be clearly written and accurate. Allow children to exchange directions and follow them.

BUNNY'S UPS AND DOWNS (Reading—Character Study) Reproducible 46 helps children focus on how a character feels and how these feelings relate to his or her actions. Tell children they can refer to the book as they answer the questions on the reproducible. Encourage children to write complete sentences for their answers.

◼ More Cross-Curricular Activities

MAPS, MAPS, AND MORE MAPS (Social Studies) Round up and bring to class, or have children bring in, different kinds of maps. Allow children to study these maps. Ask them to tell you what each map is used for. How are the maps similar? How are they different? Can students name other maps that would be good to have? Put these maps on display in your classroom.

MAKE A SCHOOL MAP (Social Studies) Take children on a walking tour of the school building. Have children jot down notes on the classrooms they pass and where the gym, library, principal's office, and auditorium are located. When children return to the classroom, have them draw and label a map of the school. Students can either work on individual school maps, or if they work in small groups, each group can take a different section of the school. Post the finished maps on a bulletin board for children to refer to when they leave the classroom.

Where Is Mrs. Walker?

Cut out Bunny.
Put her in Ms. Darcy's room.
Then follow the directions to get
Bunny to Mrs. Walker's room.

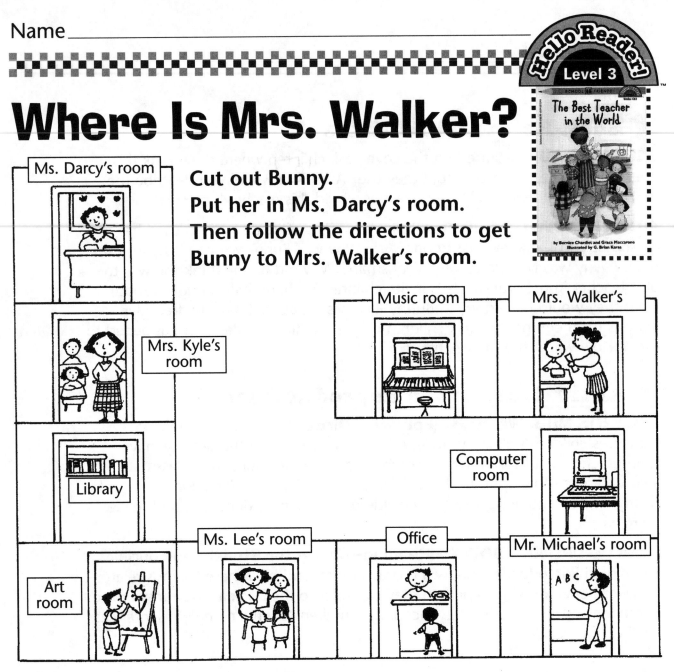

Ms. Darcy's room

Mrs. Kyle's room

Library

Art room

Music room

Mrs. Walker's

Computer room

Ms. Lee's room

Office

Mr. Michael's room

1. Take Bunny to the library.
   What room did you pass? _____

2. Now take Bunny from the library to
   Ms. Lee's room. Did you pass the office? _____

3. Take Bunny from Ms. Lee's room to the
   computer room. How many rooms did you pass? _____

4. Now find Mrs. Walker's room and put Bunny in it.
   Describe where Mrs. Walker's room is.

_____

REPRODUCIBLE 45

Hello Reader!
Level 3

The Best Teacher
in the World

by Bernice Chardiet and Grace Maccarone
Illustrated by G. Brian Karas

Bunny's Ups and Downs

Answer these questions.

1. How did Bunny feel when Ms. Darcy chose her to take the note to

   Mrs. Walker? _____

2. How did Bunny feel when Raymond called her Bunny Rabbit?

   _____

3. How did Bunny feel when she was alone in the hall? _____

   _____

4. How did Bunny feel when Mrs. Kyle's class stared at her? _____

   _____

5. How did Bunny feel when she heard Ms. Darcy reading her

   favorite story? _____

6. How did Bunny feel when she lied to Ms. Darcy? _____

   _____

7. How did Bunny feel when she told the truth? _____

   _____

THE HELLO READER! ACTIVITY BOOK   SCHOLASTIC PROFESSIONAL BOOKS

That Fat Hat

About This Book

Emma likes to be very stylish and always does what is "in" at the moment. This causes her some trouble with her best friend, Lou Lou. Emma refuses to go to lunch at the Lapping Cat restaurant if Lou Lou wears her fat hat. Fat hats are no longer "in"; everyone is now wearing small hats. So Emma and Lou Lou part company. By the end of the book, Emma learns her lesson: she doesn't have to be like everyone else. It is more important to be true to herself.

Themes

This book works well with these themes: **All About Me, Friendship, Problem Solving, Identity,** and **Conflict Resolution.**

Meet the Author and Illustrator

Joanne Barkan enjoys creating different kinds of books for young children. She is the author of two successful board book series for Cartwheel Books—*Glow in the Dark Books,* which include *A Very Scary Ghost Book, A Very Scary Haunted House, A Very Scary Jack O'Lantern,* and *A Very Scary Witch Story.* Also *Sparkle and Glow Books,* which include *Lost Little Bunny, Tooth Fairy Magic, A Very Merry Santa Claus Story,* and *A Very Merry Snowman Story.*

   Maggie Swanson is not only a children's book illustrator but has used her artistic talents doing magazine illustrations as well. She has contributed to *Sesame Street* magazine and has worked on Sesame Street licensed character books for Random House and Western Publishing.

Book-Related Activities

BEFORE READING Ask children why they think the author named this book *That Fat Hat.* (*Elicit responses such as: the words rhyme; it's a funny idea;* That Fat Hat *also rhymes with the word* cat; *it describes the big hat on the cover.*)

AFTER READING Ask: What was important about the fat hat? What was important about the flat hat? What did Emma learn? Have children tell you their favorite scenes in the book.

✥ Activities for the Reproducibles

I WEAR, YOU WEAR, I EAT, YOU EAT (Comparing and Contrasting)
Reproducible 47 helps children understand that they are individuals and that they can make up their own minds. Have children choose a friend to work with. When children finish, ask them if they wear the same thing and like the same food as their friend does. Help children realize that they can think for themselves and don't have to wear, do, or like something just because their friend does. Of course, some children may point out that they do wear or like the same things as their friend. Encourage students to realize that there is nothing wrong with that as long as they stay true to themselves and don't just follow the other person. After all, people do choose friends based on common interests, likes, and dislikes.

WHAT A HAT! (Art—Following Directions) Be sure children understand the directions before they begin the activity on Reproducible 48. Explain that they can copy a basic hat shape for A. Students will need crayons for C. Display the finished hats. Are any two exactly alike? If so, why? If not, why aren't more hats alike? To extend this activity, children might enjoy making paper or cloth hats that they can wear. Bring in scraps of fabric, glitter, buttons, fake fruit, ribbons, and so on. Have children glue or sew these items onto their hats. Then hold a Hat Fashion Parade in your classroom.

✥ More Cross-Curricular Activities

PLAY ON WORDS (Language Arts) Have children look at the illustrations in the book and read the store and street signs. Do children think these signs are funny? Why or why not? If children are having difficulty understanding any of the signs, explain the meaning of the phrase to them. Can children think of other sayings that would be funny? Then have students choose an animal, perhaps a cow, a duck, or a dog. Have children think of funny signs they could use in a town where this animal lives. Keep a running list of these phrases. Encourage children to draw a scene using the animal and one or more phrases in the background.

WHO IS EMMA? (Reading—Understanding Character) Hold a class discussion. Do children like Emma? Do children think it would be good to be like Emma? Why or why not? Were they pleased that Emma changed at the end of the book? This might be a good time to discuss what a fad is. Have students give examples of current fads. Do children always want whatever the latest fad is—in toys, clothes, accessories, music? Why?

I Wear, You Wear, I Eat, You Eat

What do you like to wear? Draw a picture here.

What does your friend like to wear? Draw a picture here.

What is your favorite food? Draw a picture here.

What is your friend's favorite food. Draw a picture here.

REPRODUCIBLE 47

Name_____

What a Hat!

Choose one kind of hat from A.
Choose two things to put on the hat from B.
Choose a color from C.

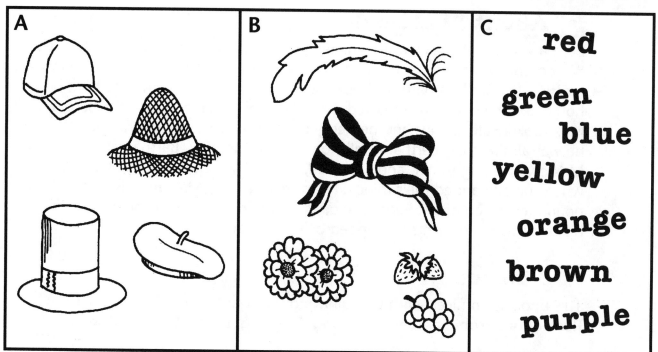

A	B	C
		red
		green
		blue
		yellow
		orange
		brown
		purple

Draw a picture of your hat.

Who's Afraid of the Big, Bad Bully?

■ About This Book

Bertha was big. Bertha was mean. Everyone was scared of big, mean Bertha. But no one was more scared than Max. Max did everything he could to avoid crossing Big Bertha's path. He took the long way to school and the long way home, and he never, ever walked down Dandelion Lane, where Big Bertha lived. Max took karate lessons and he begged his parents to buy him a dog, but still he was afraid of Big Bertha. Finally, one day at the park, Bertha demanded that Max give his dog to her, and Max said, "No!" The other kids followed suit when she demanded their things. From that day on, Max and his friends were no longer scared of Big Bertha. And, as it turned out, once everyone stopped being so scared of her, she stopped being so scary.

■ Themes

This book fits in nicely with the following themes: **Friendship, Conflict Resolution, Problem Solving, Facing Challenges,** and **Communities.**

■ Meet the Author and Illustrator

Teddy Slater knows how to communicate with young children. She chooses both humorous and serious subjects and especially likes to write about real problems that children have. That's why she researched and found out the latest information from child psychologists about the best way to handle a bully—a common childhood problem. Among her other easy-to-read books are these *Hello Readers!*—*The Bunny Hop, N-O Spells No!,* and *The Wrong-Way Rabbit.*

  Pat Porter's realistic style of illustration helped to bring Bertha the bully as well as Max, his friends, and Fang alive. The school in the book is the one Pat Porter went to as a young child—Clinton School in Maplewood, New Jersey. Porter has illustrated 24 books. Her latest one for Scholastic Inc. is *If You Lived at the Time of the Great San Francisco Earthquake.*

◼ Book-Related Activities

BEFORE READING Choose a volunteer to read the title of the book. Does this title sound familiar to children? *(Help children realize that this title is a take-off on the question "Who's afraid of the big, bad wolf?" from* Little Red Riding Hood.*)* Ask children to explain what they think is happening on the cover.

AFTER READING Now that kids have read the book, can they explain the cover better?

◼ Activities for the Reproducibles

CHANGES (Reading—Understanding Character) Reproducible 49 helps children understand the characters in the story and also to see that characters often grow and change during a story. This book touches on a fairly common childhood experience. Do children sympathize with Max? Can they give reasons as to why Bertha is a bully? Have children share their ideas.

WHAT HAPPENS WHEN? (Cause and Effect) Reproducible 50 gives children practice understanding cause and effect in a story. You might want to review this term with children before they begin. Have children give examples of cause and effect from their own experiences. Write these on the chalkboard, labeling each *cause* and *effect*. Tell children they can refer to these examples as they work on this reproducible.

◼ More Cross-Curricular Activities

HOW TO HANDLE A BULLY (Critical Thinking) Hold a group discussion about bullies. Have children had any problems with bullies? How did they handle them? Jot down students' suggestions. Do children think that the kids in the story handled Bertha the right way at the end? Why or why not? When the discussion is over, children might want to compile their suggestions for handling bullies into an advice book, *How to Get Along.*

WHAT IS KARATE? (Movement) If any children take karate, judo, or tae kwon do lessons, you might have them explain what it is and show some movements. Or you could invite an instructor to speak with students. Beforehand, have students make up a list of questions they would like to ask. The instructor might demonstrate some movements.

WHAT WOULD HAVE HAPPENED IF...? (Language Arts—Writing) Have children think about what would have happened if Max did not stand up to Bertha, and Bertha walked away with Fang. Have children draw pictures and write new endings for the book. When children are finished, have them share their endings. Take a class vote. Which ending appeared to be the most realistic?

Name_____

Changes

Think about these questions.
Then write your answers.

	Beginning of Story	**End of Story**
How does Max feel about Bertha?		
How does Bertha feel about the other kids?		

THE HELLO READER! ACTIVITY BOOK   SCHOLASTIC PROFESSIONAL BOOKS

REPRODUCIBLE 49

Name_____

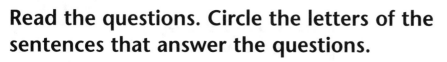

What Happens When?

Read the questions. Circle the letters of the sentences that answer the questions.

1. CAUSE: Max is scared of Big Bertha.
What EFFECTs does this have on Max?

   a. Max takes the long way to school.

   b. Max never walks on Dandelion Lane.

   c. Max stays in his father's car.

   d. Max takes karate lessons.

   e. Max tells his sister, Lila, about Big Bertha.

   f. Max gets a dog and names him Fang.

2. CAUSE: Max stands up to Big Bertha.
What EFFECTs does this have?

   a. Fang becomes an airhead dog.

   b. Becky M. stands up to Big Bertha, too.

   c. Carol Anne ignores Big Bertha.

   d. Max, Becky M., and Carol Ann become statues.

   e. Carol Anne becomes a famous baseball player.

   f. Bertha stops being so scary.

Answers to the Reproducibles

Many of the reproducibles in this book are open-ended questions or activities. Accept all reasonable responses. The following are the suggested answers to those reproducibles with specific questions.

❖❖ Level 1

REPRODUCIBLE 1:
Name That Animal
1. cow

2. pig

3. sheep

4. hen

Children should circle these words—
1. pig, cow

2. hen, pig

3. cow, sheep

4. duck, hen

REPRODUCIBLE 2:
We Speak

Children should match these sounds to these animals: peep-peep—chick, meow—cat, hissss—snake, neigh—horse, ribbit—frog, bow-wow—dog.

REPRODUCIBLE 3:
Sam Is Not Sad, Sam Is Glad

Check that students underline the endings.

-ad	-am	-ot
s<u>ad</u>	h<u>am</u>	sp<u>ot</u>
h<u>ad</u>	S<u>am</u>	forg<u>ot</u>
m<u>ad</u>	j<u>am</u>	

Children's rhymes will vary.

REPRODUCIBLE 4:
Make a Giant Sandwich
Correct order: f, a, c, b, e, d

REPRODUCIBLE 5:
Follow the Footprints

REPRODUCIBLE 6:
Whose Footprints Are These?

REPRODUCIBLE 7:
Brrr, It's Cold
boots, scarf, coat, mittens

REPRODUCIBLE 9:
Good Ideas
Children should draw a cat (taking the bow off the dog), a baby (taking the chain off the dog) and the dog playing in the mud.

REPRODUCIBLE 11:
From Seed to Flower

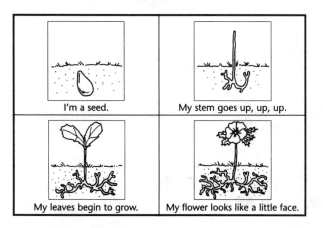

REPRODUCIBLE 12:
Here We Grow
Daisy
1. green
2. above
3. sun
4. flower
5. pretty

Carrot
1. green
2. below
3. sun
4. vegetable
5. good

REPRODUCIBLE 13:
They Come and They Go
1. middle
2. end
3. beginning

Children should draw a sad face when they first get sick.
Children should draw a happy face when they are well again.

REPRODUCIBLE 15:
"All" in the Family
-all: fall, ball, small, or meatball
Children might also include: call, hall, mall, tall, and wall.

REPRODUCIBLE 17:
We Can Do It
A worm can crawl.
A cat can jump.
A rabbit can hop.
A dog can bark.
A goldfish can swim in a bowl.
A hamster can run around.
A bird can sing.

REPRODUCIBLE 18:
Home Sweet Home
bird/birdcage; worm/container with dirt; goldfish/bowl; hamster/cage with water bottle

✦ Level 2

REPRODUCIBLE 19:
Some Silly Rhymes
1. <u>apes</u>/grapes
2. <u>bears</u>/pears
3. <u>snakes</u>/pancakes
4. <u>mice</u>/rice
5. <u>bunny</u>/honey
6. <u>fleas</u>/cheese

REPRODUCIBLE 21:
Do You Remember?
1. ultrasaurus
2. eagle
3. snake
4. elephant
5. dog
6. wolf

REPRODUCIBLE 22:
Bad Night, Good Night
small—big
gentle—fierce
tame—wild
in—out
friendly—unfriendly

REPRODUCIBLE 23:
The Facts, Please
True
2. Page 19 or 20, 21
3. Page 27
4. Page 24 or 25
6. Page 13

False
1. Page 10
5. Page 17

REPRODUCIBLE 25:
Find the Right Cure
1, 2, and 4. Any of the following:

3.

REPRODUCIBLE 27:
What Is Missing?
1. a
2. a
3. b

REPRODUCIBLE 28:
Hunt for 100
1. 99; 101
2. Responses will vary depending on when your school begins its year.
3. dollar
4. 2 hours
5. one hundred
6. 10 times
7. hot
8. Answers will vary.

REPRODUCIBLE 29:
What Happened When?
a. 3

b. 1

c. 2

d. 4

REPRODUCIBLE 30:
Wheels Go Round and Round
Children should draw wheels on the car, bus, train, bicycle, truck, baby carriage.

REPRODUCIBLE 31:
Just Do It!
1. tickled

2. tied

3. threw

4. dipped

5. made

6. jumped

Level 3

REPRODUCIBLE 38:
Friends or Foes?
Possible:
1. Cover face.

2. Wipe hands.

3. Eat regular meals.

4. Use tissue or a handkerchief.

5. Take time to flush and wash.

REPRODUCIBLE 39:
A Helen Keller Timeline
1. In 1880 a healthy baby girl is born.

2. Helen, age 2, becomes ill and loses her sight and hearing.

3. Helen starts to grow wild.

4. The Kellers talk to Dr. Alexander Bell.

5. Anne Sullivan comes to teach Helen in 1887.

6. Helen learns what "w-a-t-e-r" is.

REPRODUCIBLE 40:
Special Signs
Yes! I can read this sentence.

REPRODUCIBLE 41:
Prunella and Rosie
Prunella: 1, 3, 6, 7
Rosie: 2, 4, 5, 8

REPRODUCIBLE 42:
Say It!

2. Prunella said, "I did my best, Rosie."

3. Father said, "I'm afraid Rosie will never learn."

4. The plumber said, "I'll be right there."

5. Rosie said, "May I see the menu, please?"

REPRODUCIBLE 43:
Up and Down Words
Across

2. town

4. holiday

6. song

Down

1. popcorn

3. night

5. door

REPRODUCIBLE 45:
Where Is Mrs. Walker?

1. Mrs. Kyle's room

2. no

3. two

4. between the computer room and the music room

REPRODUCIBLE 46:
Bunny's Ups and Downs

Answers may vary but should resemble these:

1. Bunny felt proud and happy.

2. Bunny didn't care. She was too happy and proud.

3. Bunny felt sad.

4. Bunny was embarrassed.

5. Bunny wished she was inside the classroom.

6. Bunny felt bad. (Bunny felt sick.)

7. Bunny felt much better. (Bunny felt happy.)

REPRODUCIBLE 48:
What a Hat!

Check that children follow directions correctly when drawing their hats.

REPRODUCIBLE 49:
Changes

Beginning: Max doesn't like Bertha and is afraid of her. Bertha is mean to the other kids and bullies them.

Ending: Max stands up to Bertha and is no longer afraid of her. Bertha gets along with other kids. She doesn't seem so big and mean and unfriendly.

REPRODUCIBLE 50:
What Happens When?

Children should circle the letters of the following sentences.

1. a, b, d, f

2. b, c, f